Praise for *Stepping Aside, Moving Ahead*

"Steve Harper helps all of us in tr   His
book not only helps us make this   iers.
It is an excellent tool for baby boo   reat
significance in living our legacy of
—*Clayto*   *osity,*
United Methodist Church of the Resurrection, Leawood, KS; author,
Propel: Good Stewardship, Greater Generosity from Abingdon Press

"It's easy to say 'I wish I had read this book five years ago,' but it's true. Steve has brought together the practical and the spiritual, the personal and the professional dynamics of preparing for retirement in this delightful, readable collection of letters. He touches sensitive nerves and warms the spirit at the same time. For the host of baby boomer preachers like me who now face this next phase of life, Steve has offered us a guidebook for the journey."
—*John E. Harnish, retired pastor and Associate General Secretary,*
Board of Higher Education and Ministry, UMC

"Stepping Aside, Moving Ahead addresses a key area that many pastors and lay leaders fail to understand and discuss openly and provides a great resource to open the discussion with pastors as they are considering (or should be considering) retirement. Harper's insights will help clergy celebrate stepping aside as they pass the baton to the next generation of leaders."
—*Darrel Riley, Superintendent Southeast Region, Free Methodist Church*

"Steve Harper has the uncanny gift of translating deep spirituality into the day-to-day context of life. So as one facing retirement in the near future, I'm all ears. With this book he has captured the big issue and fears I face. It's a much-needed masterpiece."
—*Daryl L. Smith, Associate Professor, Asbury Theological Seminary,*
Florida Dunnam Campus

"Steve Harper writes with intentionality and wisdom about what it means to step aside and move ahead into retirement. In the style of C. S. Lewis's *The Screwtape Letters*, Harper shares a thoughtful, systematic, and practical reflection on retirement for clergy. He presents this gift to us as a teacher, spiritual director, colleague, and friend!"
—*Wayne D. Wiatt, Director, Office of Clergy Excellence,*
Florida Conference, UMC

Other Books by Steve Harper from Abingdon Press
Five Marks of a Methodist
For the Sake of the Bride

Products by Magrey deVega with Steve Harper
Five Marks of a Methodist: Participant Guide
Five Marks of a Methodist: Leader Guide
Five Marks of a Methodist: DVD

STEPPING
ASIDE
MOVING
AHEAD

Spiritual and Practical Wisdom for Clergy Retirement

Steve Harper

Nashville

STEPPING ASIDE, MOVING AHEAD:
SPIRITUAL AND PRACTICAL WISDOM FOR CLERGY RETIREMENT

Copyright © 2016 by Abingdon Press

All rights reserved.

This book is printed on acid-free paper.

Library of Congress Cataloging-in-Publication Data

Names: Harper, Steve, 1947- author.
Title: Stepping aside, moving ahead : spiritual and practical wisdom for
  clergy retirement / Steve Harper.
Description: First [edition]. | Nashville, Tennessee : Abingdon Press, 2016.
  Includes bibliographical references.
Identifiers: LCCN 2015050506 (print) | LCCN 2016000408 (ebook) | ISBN
  9781501810480 (binding: pbk.) | ISBN 9781501810497 (E-book)
Subjects: LCSH: Clergy--Retirement.
Classification: LCC BV4382 .H37 2016 (print) | LCC BV4382 (ebook) | DDC
  253/.208696--dc23
LC record available at http://lccn.loc.gov/2015050506

16 17 18 19 20 21 22 23 24 25—10 9 8 7 6 5 4 3 2 1
MANUFACTURED IN THE UNITED STATES OF AMERICA

For Jeannie,
Who walks the retirement phase of life with me,
Hand in hand and with love,
As always

Contents

CONTENTS

Introduction

My dad described his aging process this way: "It took me fifty years to be fifty, but it only took me fifteen minutes to be eighty." As I age and live into retirement, his words have become real for me. It is amazing how quickly time passes. Obviously, no one gets older more quickly than anyone else. But when we are the ones experiencing the aging journey, it *seems* as though we have arrived prematurely. Coming to retirement feels the same way.

Approximately ten thousand people retire daily in the United States, straining social networks and government programs to absorb and process the reality. Many of this daily number are clergy. In fact, the clergy demographic is on the "older" side. Our likes are retiring in large numbers, with more on the way. Moreover, as part of the new elderly, we will live longer in retirement than previous generations have done. We must not simply slip into retirement; we must prepare and plan for it.

Doing so quickly reveals retirement to be a profoundly spiritual experience—one that touches the entirety of our humanity—spirit, soul, and body, as Paul put it in 1 Thessalonians 5:23. For most of us, these three dimensions of existence will not get to retirement age in equally good shape. Retirement thus becomes a challenge to bring together the totality of our personhood in ways that enable us to step aside and yet move ahead. Retirement presents the same challenge as every stage of life: how to live abundantly.

But we clergy must deal with the leadership dynamics associated with retirement. We have become accustomed to being in the forefront. People have looked to us for guidance and help in all sorts of ways. This is true not only for pastors in local churches but also for a variety of other ministries where we have functioned as leaders. The prospect of no longer having others to lead is a formidable challenge, causing some to keep on going, fearing that a loss of position will mean a loss of life. This fear strikes particularly hard at any who have lived with an "I am what I do" identity.

For all these dynamics and more, I have written this book for those of us who approach retirement with "fightings and fears within, without" but who also come to it believing that every age and stage of life is sacred.[1] To be honest, I hesitated to write this book because I have not been retired for long. But that is the very reason Abingdon Press encouraged me to write it—to produce a book that contains memories and meditations that attend the years leading up to retirement and those immediately following it.[2] To write this way means I am a fellow traveler with you, a retirement pilgrim still forming my life for the long haul. The words here are wet clay.

As you may have noticed, I have chosen a letter format for the book. Letters have been classic media for spiritual guidance in the past. I hope they will do so now. For one thing, letters are short enough to be focused reflections on specific topics, not extended treatments of a subject like a traditional chapter would be. I believe that a formative approach to retirement requires this little-by-little

---

1. Charlotte Eilliott, "Just as I Am, Without One Plea," *The United Methodist Hymnal* (Nashville: The United Methodist Publishing House, 1989), 357.
2. There are many good books about retirement written by people who have lived farther into older adulthood. I have provided some in a reading list at the end of this book.

approach. But for another thing, letters are documents that can be read and reread, with increasing benefit. Letters can be savored. Letters create a meditative mind-set. They are spiritual formation documents.

I use the name Chris because it is a name given to women as well as to men. I want this book to include us all. But I also realize that I am a man, so I am sure there will be ways in which my ideas will need to be translated into the experience of a female clergyperson. I only hope that I will write in ways that will make any applications to your life and ministry possible.

Because of my many years teaching spiritual formation, I view this book as a *spirituality* of retirement. This not only taps my expertise but also fits my personal experience and the experience of others who find retirement to be a deep matter of soul. But in calling it a spirituality of retirement, I must emphasize that it is a book that includes every aspect of life. This is not a narrowly religious book. Spirituality is reality, or it is not spirituality. A spiritual formation book about retirement must be broad as well as deep. It must reveal Emmanuel—God with us—in retirement, as always. We can only step aside and move ahead if we are guided by the One who knows our way better than we do.

The Opening Letter

Dear Chris,

It is good to hear from you. Yes, I remember you—the classes you took with me in seminary and the conversations we had outside of class while you were a student. Those were good times. I confess that I am surprised to learn you are nearing retirement. Time passes quickly. I can only imagine how much God has used you for good during your years of ordained ministry.

I am grateful to have you reach out to me with respect to your retirement. You are wise in paying attention to this transition in advance of it. To postpone consideration of retirement can make us more reactive than responsive, which only increases the likelihood that we will not make our best decisions. I commend your foresight.

Chris, I am glad to learn that you and your spouse are talking about your retirement together.[1] You will find your spouse's wisdom to be foundational and motivational in your own deliberations. Jeannie has been, as always, my best guide and supporter as I have moved into retirement. I hope you will also reach out to others for counsel, because there is no one-size-fits-all pattern for retiring. I trust you know folks who have retired well. They can give you additional

---

1. If you are reading this book as a single clergyperson, I hope you will find a soul friend to talk with. You should not do this by yourself.

important perspective. But I accept your invitation to be of whatever help I can be.

I like your phrase "a spirituality of retirement." My own experience, combined with others I know, shows that both the consideration of retirement and the early living into it is a profound phase of the Christian spiritual life. You are on target in bringing your whole self to retirement, and that includes family dynamics and everything else, for that matter.

As we exchange letters, please know that I am not prescribing a one-size-fits-all plan for you. Life doesn't work that way, and neither does retirement. Instead, I hope to be *descriptive*, not prescriptive. My story will not be your story. But I agree with Frederick Buechner that our individual lives manifest universality.[2]

Chris, thanks for getting in touch. I am looking forward to reconnecting, walking with you, and learning from you. Abundant living is ahead of you, as it always is.

Blessings!
Steve

---

2. Frederick Buechner, *The Sacred Journey* (New York: Harper & Row, 1982), 6.

It's in the Bible

Dear Chris,

I am not surprised to learn that some have responded to your planning to retire by saying that the Bible doesn't teach it. Thankfully, most you talked with responded lightheartedly, but even underneath their touch of humor there may at least be confusion about where retirement fits into the Christian journey. Let me use this letter to tell you what I think.

I must begin by agreeing with your critics, up to a point. If they take retirement to mean a withdrawal from vital living and adopting a kind of passive life, then I think they are correct. God never calls us to become disengaged, and retirement, as I am going to write about it, is not a call to "hang it up" and coast through the remaining years of your life. What I will be pointing to in this series of letters is an ongoing journey of significance and purpose—a journey lived under the inspiration and guidance of the Holy Spirit, just as all your previous years have been. Retirement is not the cessation of activity, but only a change in it.

But having said that, I must disagree with your critics. I have found that some folks use the "it's not biblical" response as a license to keep on going through a series of reinventions of themselves. They may have quit one job, but they quickly find another one to give them a sense of significance. Simply put, they do not know how to let go. They falsely equate their role with their life and run the risk of defining it in terms of activism, and even worse, by status. This is a matter that will require further attention in our correspondence, but I mention it now because you may have fallen prey to some clergy who think that the abandonment of their professional role is tantamount to the loss of their personhood. This is a serious error.

Instead, I want you to consider some things about retirement that are in the Bible. First, the Bible does teach specifically about retirement, and it does so with respect to religious leaders. In Numbers 8:25-26, the Levites are told that at age fifty, they are to retire from their service. They are no longer to perform their previous duties. Doubtless, this prescription was related to the fact that these people were considered to be "old" in that era. In that context, the verses make it clear that these leaders were to do two things: (1) move aside so that younger people could perform the duties, and (2) support those younger persons as they did so.

The longer I ponder these two verses, the more convinced I am that they are a deep well of wisdom. For one thing, they acknowledge the aging process—something those who resist retirement often are failing to do. Second, they teach that we have our particular generation of service, and when it is passed, we should get out of the way so that younger people can have theirs. Not to do this is to create a "clog" in the pipeline of servanthood that delays younger people from having their day. Finally, these verses make clear that we do not cease serving, but rather we serve in a new way—especially through our becoming supporters of those who have moved into their time of leadership.

But that is not all the Bible reveals about retirement. We gain insight from the patriarchs and matriarchs. These men and women do not continue to do what they have always done. Rather, they begin to do new things. In the Old Testament, for example, we see older men sitting by the gate, making themselves available for conversation and counsel. In the New Testament, the apostle Paul wrote to older men and women, exhorting them to fulfill the important ministries of setting a godly example and mentoring younger men and women (Titus 2:2-5). Paul took his own advice by passing the torch of leadership to Timothy and to Titus, understanding that he had served his generation and was now to become an encourager to his two young friends who were now called to be ministers.

So, far from not teaching about retirement, I believe the Bible has a lot to say about it. It challenges any who believe they should never retire. It constructs an active view of retirement. Most of all, it offers us a farther journey into abundant living. The God of life does not have a moment when we leave life behind. But God does have a phase of life when we live differently than we have in the past. God opens the door to another room of life. Don't let your detractors talk you out of it.

Blessings!
Steve

Establishing the Vision

Dear Chris,

I am relieved to know that you look at retirement in a positive light and as part of the human journey. I will not write a lot about the aging process in general because it's not my expertise. There are good books that can get you started along this more generic, human development pathway.[1]

I will focus our letters, exploring the several years leading up to retirement and the several following it, in relation to Christian formation. I believe I can be most helpful to you by doing this.

But you must be aware that my understanding of spirituality is comprehensive, not something restricted to the "religious" domain. Human development and spiritual formation are intertwined. Retirement is a whole-life experience. To be human is to be made in the image of God, and everything else revolves around that. Retirement is profoundly spiritual because it is another opportunity to become fully human. Older adulthood is sacred.

It is the fallen world that makes "youthfulness" appear to be the ideal stage, forcing children to look older than they are, and trying to keep adults looking younger than they are. This is an artificial, cosmetic understanding of life—not the one God wants us to have.

---

1. At the end of this book, I have provided a bibliography that contains both general human development resources, as well as some that connect our journey to the Christian spiritual life.

Every phase of our life continues the life principle. I am so glad you see it that way.

This enables us to build a spiritual house regarding retirement. I have found the threefold formation paradigm proposed by Richard Foster in one of his books, *Life With God* and also in the *The Life With God Bible*.[2] Foster believes that formation occurs in relation to three words: *vision, intention,* and *means.* I agree with him, and I will make use of these three concepts in the opening round of our correspondence.

Let's begin with the *vision* that gives rise to retirement. Fundamentally, it is the conviction that life goes on. I have already alluded to this, but I repeat it now as part of the necessary vision. It is the conviction that abundant living (John 10:10) is available all along the life path. E. Stanley Jones bore witness to this by showing how each phase of his life had been meaningful and how he was confident that the future would be as well.[3] The formative vision for retirement is fueled by anticipation—by the conviction that until our final breath, we are made to experience things that no previous time of life has given us.

The vision for retirement continues in the awareness that life is lived from the inside out. We do not pit the inward against the outward, but we do recognize that the call is to *be* someone before we do something. Or to say it in the classical sense, character (virtue) is the foundation for conduct (voyage). John Wesley recognized this when he launched the early Methodist movement. He created Methodism's foundation with two documents: *The Character of a Methodist*

---

2. Richard Foster, *Life With God* (San Francisco: HarperOne, 2008); *The Life With God Bible* (San Francisco: HarperOne, 2005). For more about this and the Renovare ministry, go to www.renovare.org.

3. E. Stanley Jones, *A Song of Ascents: A Spiritual Autobiography* (Nashville: Abingdon Press, 1968), 367.

in 1742, and *The General Rules of the United Societies* in 1743.[4] In this regard, he was a classical spiritual guide, inviting people onto a journey marked by personal and social holiness—holiness of heart and life.

Similarly, retirement affects us inwardly and outwardly. Retirement is to be a matter of significant soul work—whole-life work that develops our character and designs conduct. Both aspects are developed in relation to the fruit of the Spirit: love, joy, peace, patience, kindness, goodness, faithfulness, gentleness, and self-control (Gal 5:22-23). These constitute what Christians have often referred to as the *virtuous life*.

Retirement gives us the opportunity to engage these nine dynamics in new ways, and to do it through the ordinary routines of everyday living. This more natural, casual, and unhurried manifestation of the fruit of the Spirit helps overcome a production-oriented life that we can so easily become used to as clergy. We find that opportunities for holy conversation increase.

Chris, I have found this to be true in the early years of my retirement. I no longer live "by the clock," and I have almost no deadline-driven assignments. I am free to pace myself in relation to another rhythm of life. It is refreshing and flat-out fun!

Blessings!
Steve

---

4. Both of these treatises are found in any edition of Wesley's works. Contemporary restatements of them have been done by me (*Five Marks of a Methodist*, re-presenting *The Character of a Methodist*), and by Bishop Rueben Job (*Three Simple Rules*, re-presenting the *General Rules*). Both are available from Abingdon Press, along with accompanying individual group guides and video presentations.

Engaging the Intention

Dear Chris,

Thanks for affirming the vision I offered. You have always struck me as a person who never allowed yourself to become role defined, much less to live in the past. Using Foster's paradigm, we can now move on to explore intention.

Foster essentially means using our will to make the vision real and alive. I am pretty sure he inherited this idea from his mentor Dallas Willard, who emphasized the place and importance of the will in spiritual formation, thus preventing it from becoming a form of quietism and passivity. Intention prevents life from becoming overly conceptual or theoretical. John Wesley called it practical divinity.

But it is important to recognize that intention is not the same as function. That comes later in the formative process, even though we tend to rush to it in our activistic, performance-oriented, how-to culture. We are especially prone to this in North American Christianity where so much of ministry has revolved around programming and productivity.[1] It is what Thomas Merton warned about when he called activism a form of violence.[2] By contrast, living with intention

---

1. Eugene Peterson has written about this in many of his books. One of the earliest was *Working the Angles* (Grand Rapids: Eerdmans, 1987), but he continued to emphasize it in later volumes like *The Jesus Way* (Grand Rapids: Eerdmans, 2007).

2. Thomas Merton, *Conjectures of a Guilty Bystander* (Garden City, NY: Image Books, 1968), 86.

is moving in congruence with the initial vision, with what the Bible calls an inclined heart (Josh 24:23).

When applied to retirement, it means we dispose ourselves toward the desired vision. We "incline our heart to the Lord" so that the vision can become a reality. Over the years, I have used three words to refer to the fundamental dispositions of the ministerial heart: *learner, leader,* and *light.* I'm not sure I ever shared this view with you, so let me do so now. This is not a conceptual detour, but rather signposts that guide our life journey.

Chris, I don't have to tell you about the phase of being a learner. I remember your love of learning. I am sure you heard me say more than once that, as a student, you should never apologize for being essentially in a learning phase. In fact, I'm sure you also heard me say that the word *disciple* means "learner." The ordination process included an emphasis upon it. We call it theological education. But the fact is, we never stop learning.

But we do move into the phase of being a leader. For you, it began even while you were in seminary, and it has been the focal phase of your life for decades. Perhaps you will recall that I always described leadership in more ways than our ministerial role. We also lead as a spouse, as a parent, as a community person, and in multiple other ways. This is your calling, but as I said earlier, when we come to retirement it can be an obstacle more than a blessing if we cannot let go of being leaders. But because this is not a problem for you, we can move on.

In terms of spiritual formation, it means we become lights. Thankfully, I have had good models for learning this. From them I have seen real-life examples of how important it is to become encouragers and supporters—of becoming those who bear witness to the reality of abundant living in older adulthood. Chris, there comes the time when we are meant to be lights for those coming along behind us. I cannot overestimate the importance of becoming a light, and I don't believe we have enough of them today. I have heard younger clergy verbalize their wish that they could connect with older ones to receive support and counsel. What Eugene Peterson called "the ministry of small talk" is sorely needed.[3]

Chris, do not skip over or rush past this second formative principle. Engaging your intention opens the door to the many practical aspects of retirement. It does so by reminding us that we are doing the right thing—that there is life even after we take our name off the church sign.

Blessings!
Steve

---

3. Eugene Peterson, *The Contemplative Pastor: Returning to the Art of Spiritual Direction* (Waco: Word, 1989), 117–22.

Enacting the Means

Dear Chris,

You raise an interesting point in your struggle with the phrase "finishing well." I believe Foster's paradigm helps us do this, but I do not believe that retirement is a *finish*, but is more nearly an altered continuation. I don't even view death as a finish. I believe that in ways we cannot describe, our lives here are a preparation for a life that is beyond time. If that is true, how could we ever see retirement as an ending? We are made for eternity! How we live here and now sets a trajectory for it.

At the same time, you are correct in recognizing that whatever we mean by "finishing well" it includes a host of details—some small, some large. And I think you are also correct in connecting this to our Wesleyan theology of practical divinity, where we must eventually turn theory into practice. This is what our Christian predecessors called ordinary holiness. Using Foster's paradigm it means that when vision and intention are in place, we can move into the third phase called means.

But I do want to use this letter to put the third of Richard Foster's elements into the picture—the element of means. We enact our convictions. I think we are in a good place to direct our correspondence in that direction. When a tree is rooted, it can bear fruit. When we are grounded through vision and intention, we can discern good means for living in retirement. But prior to any specific details, we must establish the basic design.

I believe we do this in relation to the two great commandments—loving God and loving others. Whatever else retirement brings about, these two elements must be in play. We are called to live in ways that glorify God and honor others. Through holiness of heart we glorify God, and through holiness of life, we honor others. I like to think of it in terms of breathing. When we inhale spiritually we "oxygenate" our lives with the love of God. When we exhale spirituality we "embody" that love for the sake of others. The attitudes and actions we use in doing this are many, and we will be looking at some of them.

For now, I want to make it clear that even the *means* are rooted in personhood, not performance. The people I know who have moved into retirement the best are those who carry love for God and others with them. In their retirement years they seek for, and find, concrete expressions to do both. Their lives continue to be engaged in the living out of this vision. These folks tell us that we do not have to look in the rearview mirror to find life.

Blessings!
Steve

Whole-Life Retirement

Dear Chris,

Perhaps you remember I taught in class that when the hymnal is revised, I want to propose that it includes "The Hokey Pokey." Actually, I am only half-joking when I say this. As you know, the song moves from partial to complete involvement, the end coming when we put our *whole self in*. You would have to search a long time to find a better example of spiritual formation than that. The fact is, the word *salvation* means "wholeness," and no part of the Christian tradition commends half-hearted discipleship.

The ultimate icon of this is the cross. But the early Christians realized that not everyone literally dies on one, so they found other ways to describe total commitment. One of the shortest and best comes from Paul when he wrote, "Now, may the God of peace himself cause you to be completely dedicated to him; and may your spirit, soul, and body be kept intact and blameless at our Lord Jesus Christ's coming" (1 Thess 5:23). The "spirit, soul, and body" trinity was his way of telling the Thessalonians to put their whole self in. It is essentially what the Wesleyan tradition means in the phrase "entire sanctification"—what Søren Kierkegaard meant when he wrote, "Purity of heart is to will one thing."[1]

---

1. Søren Kierkegaard, *Purity of Heart Is to Will One Thing* (np: Feather Trail Press, 2009).

Chris, you will remember that this verse was one of the pivotal passages over the centuries for the holy living tradition in general (with its emphasis upon holiness of heart and life) and for early Methodism in particular (with its emphasis upon entire sanctification), both of which interpreted Christian perfection not as flawless performance, but rather as purity of intention—captured by Søren Kierkegaard in his classic statement, "Purity of heart is to will one thing."[2] I think we are in a position to use the spirit, soul, and body image to talk about spiritual formation in retirement. Let's begin with spirit.[3]

The spirit is essence of who we are. It is the core of our being. It is the dimension of us that transcends time and space—the part of us that is eternal. It is intangible in its makeup, but if we honor it, the spirit influences us more than anything else. In the best sense of the word, it is why we keep desiring to "be spiritual"—not as an escape from tangible life, but as coming to have a life that is defined and directed by things unseen. One synonym for it is *intuition*.

With respect to retirement it comes into play as we become contemplative—something I once misunderstood severely but now embrace heartily. The word is made up of two parts: "con" and "template," literally meaning "with the template." This began to make sense to me when I started using computers. The computer manufacturers put templates into their machines to provide a basis and a form for many actions. They are there for our benefit. When we are "with the template"—when we are contemplative, when we operate in sync with things, we do not invent on our own.

2. Ibid.

3. In this series of letters, I have chosen not to connect the humanness of spirit, soul, and body with the Trinity, although theologically it is beneficial to do so. This threefold definition of humanity is much more than a simple comparison of it with the threefold nature of God. There is not a one-to-one correspondence between God's nature and ours. But we are made in the image of God, and so our spirit, soul, and body exist in relation to God.

We need to become contemplative with respect to retirement. We need to get in touch with the values that we believe enable us to live the way God intended. In Christian history, these were called virtues. Chris, if you are of a mind to do so, get a copy of the *Catechism of the Catholic Church*.[4] Over the centuries the Roman Church has studied and taught more about the virtuous life than many Protestant denominations have done. The *Catechism* will seed your mind and heart with more good things than I can describe here.

But for now, understand that the virtues are grouped into several key categories. The theological virtues (faith, hope, and love) are the roots from which all the others come. The cardinal virtues (prudence, justice, fortitude, and temperance) are the main ways that the theological virtues are expressed. And finally the human virtues (firm attitudes and stable dispositions) inform the intellect, inspire the will, and inform our actions. All three types of virtue are given to us by God through grace. They are the foundational life principles that help us to recognize what is good and tend toward it with wholehearted devotion.[5]

Chris, you may think that I am wandering off the path in emphasizing all this, but I assure you I am not. What the spirit invites and enables us to see are those qualities of life that make our existence sacred. As we move into retirement, we want to do all we can to be sure we are constructing our spiritual house on the good foundation. This means spending time mulling over the key elements of virtue, asking ourselves about each, "How can I use my retirement years to make these things more genuine and increasingly enacted?" Because we are not as encumbered with the pink "while you were out" notes,

---

4. It is available in both traditional and e-book formats. The volume I am using to write about the virtues is a paperback edition published by Doubleday in 1995.

5. I have found Susan Muto's book *Virtues: Your Christian Legacy* (Steubenville, OH: Emmaus Road Publishing, 2014) to be a very helpful exploration of the virtuous life.

we have the opportunity to do what Paul exhorted us to do: "If any-thing is excellent and if anything is admirable, focus your thoughts on these things: all that is true, all that is holy, all that is just, all that is pure, all that is lovely, and all that is worthy of praise" (Phil 4:8).

Chris, this is living in the spirit. It is doing what Oswald Cham-bers commended, giving our utmost for God's highest. It is allow-ing the treasures of heaven, where moth and rust do not corrupt, to invade our consciousness, infuse our conscience, and inform our character. Living in the spirit is beginning at the top, allowing the essence of the gospel to be our food and drink. I want to encourage you to begin carving out some retreat time in your schedule—time where you can go away and rest for a while, thinking about these things—doing the Hokey Pokey by putting your whole self "in" to your plans for living in retirement.

Blessings!
Steve

You've Got Soul!

Dear Chris,

It may surprise you, but I believe that when it comes to these three words (spirit, soul, and body), we are most out of touch with soul. We seem to gravitate toward the extremes. For example, some people emphasize spirit so much that we say they are heavenly minded but no earthly good. On the other hand, some people seem to be so body-oriented that the higher values of spirit hardly appear on their radar screen. This is unfortunate because it is in the domain of soul where we find the essence of our humanity—the union of spirit and body. We are not (at least on this earth) pure spirits, and we are certainly not solely bodies. We are living souls.

So, it is in the realm of the soul where we find the mediator between spirit and body. It is when we live with *soul* that we avoid the extremes of spiritism on the one hand and materialism on the other. But this is by no means as simple or easy as it sounds, because as I have just said, the pendulum of life keeps swinging from one end to the other, only temporarily passing through the soul, where God intends for us to live.

But, what is the soul? Believe me, this one word can take us into the depths of philosophy, theology, and the behavioral sciences. A consideration of soul can be complex, and overly so for our correspondence. It can also be a consideration that skews us into pop-spirituality that caters to the ego (the false self) more than Christian spirituality does. We live in a time when the redemption of the word *soul* is sorely needed.

So, back to the question: What is soul? I like to begin with the idea of consciousness. I mean that the soul is where we link the spirit and the body through the awareness of the "things above" that Paul commends and the activation of those things into thoughts, words, and deeds. The classical word for this is *animation*. The soul enables us to become animated (enlivened) by the highest and to devote our utmost to it, to borrow from Oswald Chambers again. It is in the soul where we receive the life of God and from where we then share it.

This is why the soul is immaterial in its nature but not divorced from the material. As Bernard of Clairvaux taught through his writings, the soul overlaps the unseen and the seen. It receives the unseen things of the spirit and brings them to our consciousness through the senses. It also happens in reverse: the soul makes use of our senses to bring us into consciousness of the spirit. It can happen either way. This back-and-forth rhythm creates true energy—energy we refer to as life. I think that is why Genesis 2:7 reads the way it does. When God (who is pure Spirit) connected with (breathed into) the being (body), that being became a "living soul." Where spirit and body intersect, we come alive. This is another reason why the extremes of spiritism and materialism are unable to give us life. We live where spirit and body intersect.

The soul also includes what we call the will. The soul not only receives and reveals the things of the spirit but also moves us to decide about those things and direct them into their proper places in our life. The will is where receptivity turns into response. It is what some call *mind*, where we not only think about the higher things but also determine how to live them out. This includes intelligence, but soul is more than knowledge or IQ; it includes the power of discernment and leads us to consecrate ourselves to the things of the spirit in the core of our being. Soul includes the usual means of knowing, as well as a kind of "unknowing" where we learn from things that can never be fully put into words, much less fully grasped. The soul is where mystery is allowed to exist and to influence us.

The soul is also the dimension of our existence where obedience is born and nurtured. As you know, the word *obey* comes from the root that means "listening" or "paying attention." Obedience is not simply acting; it is acting in response to what we have seen and heard. It is what our Buddhist friends call *mindfulness*. The soul uses the senses to provide us with the evidence, and then through the soulful gift of the will, we enact the highest and best, turning them into words and deeds that enrich us and others.

Chris, here is the place to transition from the soul to retirement. Taking what I wrote about spirit in the previous letter, I think that living with soul means discerning how to order our lives so that they become manifestations of our sacred values. Those values, as I said last time, come to us from spirit. But it is in the domain of soul that they are given life and direction into day-to-day specifics. Soul is where ideals and actions are blended.

We can illustrate this with the fruit of the Spirit, but I will not go through all nine dimensions now. But using love as the illustration, it is in the soul where love is turned into loving. The virtue of love (spirit) is energized by the senses in ways that make us loving people. And so too with the other eight aspects, and with everything else for that matter. In terms of spiritual formation, this is usually called meditation—what Evelyn Underhill called "mental prayer."[1]

---

1. Evelyn Underhill and Charles Lewis Slattery, *Concerning the Inner Life* (New York: E. P. Dutton & Company, 1947), 37.

It is what people usually mean when they say they are "praying about it." Contemplation is the highest form of meditation, harvesting the values and virtues of spirit so that they become nourishing to ourselves and others. In the soul, we "think about these things" and in the process of doing so, we convert revelation into responsiveness.

As we approach retirement and begin to live into it, this means continuing to ponder the domain of the spirit, and to do so in ways that turn our principles into performance. I like to think of it as what happens when we bake a cake. A conglomeration of ingredients comes out of the oven as a new food that can be eaten. The soul is the oven of transformation. In retirement we have the opportunity to mix together our deepest values, bake them in the oven of meditation, and then offer the new product as food we can use to feed ourselves and others.

Just as I encouraged you to begin scheduling retreat time to contemplate the things of the spirit, I would now move on to counsel you to include in those retreats time to consider ways you might turn your values into a voyage. Of course, your insights will be preliminary, and you must not view your predilections as requirements. But as you live with soul relative to your retirement, you will begin to connect principles with potential performances. This is the way life works. A new stage does not leave the past behind, but forms it into new ways of expressing the deepest commitments of our lives, by which we have been living for a long time.

Chris, your soul has always been the dimension of your life where you "humanize" your spirit, where you transform awareness into action. I am not asking you to do anything new, but only to apply to your retirement the same soulfulness you have been using to give your life substance and expression. As you do this, I believe it will be in your soul where your hopes and dreams for retirement begin to be transformed into possibilities that God may eventually turn into realities. And when you hold all this loosely, living with soul can actually be fun and recreative, increasing your confidence that retirement offers you the opportunity to live as fully as you ever have.

Blessings!
Steve

Body Life

Dear Chris,

On the basis of what we have said about spirit and soul, we can now turn our attention to the body. The first thing to say is that Christians are not dualists, and certainly not gnostics. We do not see the spirit as good and the body as evil. We do not disrespect the body. But we are not hedonists either; that is, we do not exalt the body beyond its place, and we certainly do not live with an "eat, drink, and be merry, for tomorrow we die" perspective. Unfortunately, we see these extremes lived out all around us by those who denigrate their bodies and those who idolize them. The Christian way is different. We consecrate the body (Rom 12:1).

We understand that our bodies are our tangible presence in the world. We do not live by our appearances, but we do live by our use of our senses. We receive much of life through sight, sound, smell, taste, and touch. We respond to what we receive through our words and deeds. Our bodies become the instrument used by our spirit and soul to incarnate our convictions through concrete actions. This is why, for example, most New Testament scholars take Paul's use of the word "bodies" in Romans 12:1 to mean more than one aspect of our existence—the culmination of the totality of who we are as human beings. But as Paul rightly notes, it all comes to bear through the body.

As with the spirit and the soul, there are too many things with respect to the body to address in one letter. I will mention only some things that seem to me to have a bearing on retirement. But I have found several to be important with respect to retirement.

The first is presence. This is a kind of throwback to what I said about being a "light" in a previous letter. But it also means that our bodies are the manifestations of the virtues we spoke about in relation to spirit. For example, if we look at our retirement as a time to manifest love, we are going to do it through our bodies as we speak loving words and express loving actions. The body is our instrument of presence.

The second thing is participation. This is an illustration of the kinds of things we referred to in the letter about soul. It is through our bodies that we animate our attitudes. It is with our bodies that we participate with others in bringing to pass what we pray almost every day, "Thy kingdom come, thy will be done, on earth as it is in heaven." Retirement is an open invitation to living in congruence with this part of the Lord's Prayer. We are freed from many of our previous responsibilities. The time we used to give to certain things is now available to enact our deepest convictions through new means. Just yesterday, for example, I talked with a retired friend who has had a heart for the poor for a long time, and he expressed that throughout the years of his ministry. But now, in retirement he has the freedom to increase his compassion in a particular ministry to the poor. I could sense his passion by the way he described this new venture, and by his *body language* as he did so.

The third dimension is preservation. Simply put, this means keeping our bodies in good shape. I have found people doing this in so many different ways that there is no one plan or program I can commend. All I can say is that reasonable care toward such things as sleep, diet, exercise, and recreation is necessary if retirement is to be all it can be. St. Francis said that the soul rides on the back of Brother Donkey, and that it can only go as far as Brother Donkey takes it. This was his way of describing the spirit/soul/body unity, with one aspect always being connected with and dependent upon another.

As I said at the beginning of our look at the body, soul, spirit paradigm, these are not three separate existences, but only three ways to describe our singular human existence. But it does mean that good care of our body will enhance and extend our life. There is mystery here, as illustrated by the fact that some who do all the right things still fall prey to disease and debilitation, while some who seemingly neglect their bodies remain healthy. But the exceptions only prove the larger rule—that caring for our body is a good thing and must not be neglected in any program of spiritual formation.

Finally, we see the body in terms of pace. Because of our over-emphasis on youthfulness in North America, we ignore (to our detriment) the fact that we are aging and that aging is part of our spiritual journey, not an enemy of it. Gerontologists often describe aging in three stages—go-go, slow-go, and no-go. If we are in reasonably good health when we retire, we can anticipate roughly a decade in each phase. Thankfully, Jeannie and I are in the go-go phase where we can do essentially whatever we want to do. But even so, it is not at the same pace as when we were younger and had so many responsibilities calling for our involvement. Even as we go-go, we can already recognize that our mind-set toward activism is changing, and that we enjoy and thrive on extended periods of silence and solitude.

Dr. Susan Muto has referred to this as "the pace of grace."[1] Unfortunately, as she points out, it is a pace many do not even know

---

1. Susan Muto, *Meditation in Motion* (Garden City, NY: Image Books, 1986), 34. Chapter 2, "Living Harmoniously," unpacks the phrase in a very helpful way; the whole book is an invitation to live transformatively. It is a gem.

grace has, a pace we are often strangers to, and a pace that we violate too much even when we know about it. But it is there, and we do well to connect with it as soon as we can. It is not the same pace at every stage of life, and the challenge is to find the pace of grace most appropriate for each stage of life. This also includes honoring the daily cycle, which does not call for the same pace 24/7. The people I know who have lived well in retirement are those who have found their pace, and who have not tried to continue to live at the same pace they did previously. It is what Joan Chittister has referred to as living by a divine plan when there is no career plan.[2]

Chris, all this happens in and through our bodies. They are the receptors of revelation and the responders to it. They are the instruments through which intake becomes outflow. They are the ways the Word continues to be made flesh in the unique time and place where each of us finds ourselves. Take good care of Brother Donkey, and you will be in for a good ride, even in retirement.

Blessings!
Steve

---

2. Joan Chittister, *The Gift of Years* (New York: BlueBridge, 2008), ix.

The Integrative Factor

Dear Chris,

You are right in saying that spirit, soul, and body are a "mixture" that combine to give us life. And you are right in suggesting that every mixture has to be stirred by a spoon. Spiritual formation is no different. As far as I am concerned, the stirring spoon is prayer.[1] This is more than me simply saying, "Chris, pray about retirement." That's stating the obvious, and I know you are doing so. The stirring spoon that I have in mind is captured in Paul's exhortations to "pray continually" (1 Thess 5:17) and "train yourself for a holy life" (1 Tim 4:7). So, we are ready to ask, "How then shall we pray?"

Of course, specific times of prayer are important. In all my studies, I have not run across a single saint who failed to develop some kind of prayer time. But the ways they did so are many and various. The thread running through all the variations is devotion to ongoing communion with God. The important thing is the disposition of your heart, not the details of your plan. But even with this freedom, we will still order our prayer life to include fixed times to pray.

---

1. In this regard, I have found James Finley's book *Merton's Palace of Nowhere: A Search for God through Awareness of the True Self* (Notre Dame, IN: Ave Maria Press, 1978) to be very helpful. In it he shows how prayer was the integrating and transforming element in Merton's spirituality and in his understanding of the Christian spiritual life. There are many parallels with Wesley's understanding of prayer as the chief means of grace.

What I find when working with clergy is that we often have to jettison a ceremonial view of prayer for a deeply personal one. Almost without realizing it, we became "prayer machines"—able to come up with a prayer for almost any occasion. We were the go-to prayer people in a crowd. If those prayers were genuine, there is nothing wrong with that. The problem is that the clerical prayer life can drift into the public expressions of prayer. But in retirement, almost all of our public praying comes to an end. Our life of prayer, however, does not.

This means that our praying expresses the realities of life. For example, when we are insecure, we pray, "God, I feel like everything I have become familiar with is changing." When our transition from one phase of life to another feels more like a train wreck than a well-ordered journey, we say, "God, I am a mess right now." You get the idea. The honesty that you bring to your prayers will often be the degree that you can celebrate the certainties and confront the challenges. It's another expression that spirituality is reality.

When I consider this kind of formative praying, I often think about Ignatius of Loyola's *Spiritual Exercises*.[2] I am not suggesting that you rush out and get a copy of the book and begin following the path it prescribes. It is a heavyweight plan to practice. But the essence of it can give you good spiritual counsel that can serve you well as you approach retirement. Ignatius's overarching teaching is that whatever means you use, they should be producing a sense of life in you. I remember Richard Foster saying long ago, if your practice of the spiritual disciplines is not life-giving, something is wrong. I would say the same thing about pre-retirement prayer. Don't fret over finding the perfect practice; just make use of the ones that have served you well over the years of your life. You will likely find them

---

2. This book is available in a host of e-book and traditional book formats.

able to do the same now. The idea of spiritual *exercise* that Ignatius commended is really his way of saying that we must not be hit-and-miss in this formative endeavor; rather, we must be devoting ourselves to prayer in ways that lead us step-by-step into discernment, discovery, and decision making.[3]

Drawing on the singular intent of the Ignatian method, I would encourage you to use your praying to establish the foundation of conviction that retirement is an equally valid period of time in which we experience abundant life. I would encourage you to use prayer as a means to kindle a desire to live for God in ways that reflect the two great commandments. I would encourage you to use prayer as a practice to "ask, seek, and knock" with respect to your dreams and visions for continuing to be a servant in the kingdom of God.

In all of this, I would urge you to let Charles Wesley's phrase "if to the right or left I stray, that moment Lord, reprove" help you cultivate a spirit of sensitivity and responsiveness to God's little-by-little guidance.[4] Prayer is to the soul what experimentation is to science. One facet of this means knowing in advance that we are not always going to get it right, and that the life of prayer not only permits but encourages U-turns on the holiness highway. Thomas Edison, for example, failed many times in his attempt to make a lightbulb. Praying about retirement will include starts and stops in the discernment experience. The kind of praying I am commending in this letter is one that says "oops" as well as "hallelujah."

Chris, I honestly believe that if you make prayer your stirring spoon, you will find that the ingredients we have looked at in the

---

3. I have written about this kind of praying in my book *Walking in the Light* (Nashville: Upper Room Books, 2014).

4. Charles Wesley, "I Want a Principle Within," in *A Collection of Hymns, for the Use of the People called Methodists,* John Wesley (London: Wesley-Methodist Book-Room, 1889), hymn 308, http://www.ccel.org/w/wesley/hymn/jwg03/jwg0308.html.

previous letters will begin to mix together in ways that will provide you with good food for the journey. And as with any good baker, you will add your own touches to the cake that will make it have a taste and décor that suits your life and the particular phase called retirement.

Blessings!
Steve

Leaving a Legacy

Dear Chris,

You ask, "Do you know anyone who has retired well?" I know you do not mean someone who has retired without stress or strain. I know you mean in relation to the spiritual formation principles we have been exploring. You have every right to ask this question; it is a good one.

In this letter I will offer you the example of my good friend and longtime mentor David McKenna. I had the privilege of serving in his administration while he was president of Asbury Theological Seminary. Throughout his tenure there I respected his authenticity and creativity. Without even knowing it, he taught me a lot about being a disciple in general and a leader in particular. It was only when he came to his time of retirement that I realized he had another role to play in my life: setting a good example for me and giving me wise counsel as I approached and lived into my retirement.

I was present when he announced his retirement to the seminary community. We were surprised, because there was nothing to indicate that he needed to retire. He was well loved, was successful in his leadership, and still had good years of service ahead of him. But he stood before us in chapel one day to say he would retire a little over a year after this announcement. And when the time came, he made good on his promise. Chris, let me share with you some of the important things that his actions modeled for me.

First, I realized that there has to be a last day. Some people deliberately ignore that reality, pushing retirement into an undetermined future. But no one serves forever. We have the ability to recall our first day on the job, but none of us can know then when our last day will be. But there will be one. There is always a last day. I learned from David that it is the wiser thing to claim that reality rather than letting it take possession of you. Failing to do this causes some to come to their last day against their will, perhaps through disease or by the will of the community around them. No matter the reason, it almost always turns the moment of retirement sour in some way, and likely the days leading up to it as well. Far better, I learned from David to anticipate a last day rather than have it thrust upon you.

Second, his announcement set in motion a healthy succession cycle. This is especially important in institutions. People need time to adjust to the transition that a retirement announcement creates. And there needs to be a generous period of time when people can form good teams and committees to make the change beneficial to themselves, as well as to the exiting and entering leaders. In the same way that leaders find it difficult to accept the fact of their last day, those they serve struggle too. Communities wrestle, fear, and grieve. Giving everyone plenty of time to settle in to the new reality and plan for the future is an act of generosity on the exiting leader's part.

Third, David's announcement solidified in him a decision he could so easily have deferred. I did not realize this until later, when Jeannie and I had dinner with him and his wife, Janet. It happened to coincide with my leaving the seminary to go to the Upper Room in Nashville, so part of the evening was given over to our respective "exits." David surprised me by saying, "If I had not announced my retirement last year, I might not be retiring now. For everything in me urges me to continue." Honestly, I had not thought about it that way before, but I have never stopped viewing it that way since. The easiest commitment to break is one that no one else knows you have made. Announcing his retirement was as necessary for him (perhaps more so) than it was for those of us who heard it.

Chris, I could go on. But happily, David has put these kinds of things and more into an excellent book, *The Leader's Legacy*.[1] I would encourage you to get it. Providentially, it came out the year Jeannie and I took a sabbatical, and we used a portion of our sabbatical time to begin talking about the eventuality of stepping down from the administrative position I held at the time, and the inevitability of our complete retirement that would likely follow shortly thereafter. We took David's book with us as we traveled across the country, and when we arrived in Seattle, I had the opportunity to thank him for the book and to have another good conversation with him. By then, he and Janet were well into their retirement years, and his initial offerings were now being tested and seasoned with the passing of time. I am glad to tell you that David wrote a second book, *Retirement Is Not for Sissies*.[2] I made good use of it as well in approaching my retirement and living into the early years of it. Consider getting it too.

Chris, I have no doubt that I will be sharing further insights from both of these books, because other things David did and said have made their way into my life. If I had to boil it down to one thing, I would say that I have learned from David McKenna the critical difference between making an impact and leaving a legacy. If we aim to make an impact, we put the emphasis on the place we are now serving—forgetting that institutions inevitably change and move on,

---

1. David McKenna, *The Leader's Legacy* (Newberg, OR: Barclay Press, 2006).
2. David McKenna, *Retirement Is Not for Sissies* (Newberg, OR: Barclay Press, 2008).

eventually being made up of people who never even knew us, much less lived under the influence of our ministry. But if we aim to leave a legacy, our emphasis is on the people whom we have served. They continue to live and serve long after we are gone. Institutions do not remember former leaders, and we should not expect them to. But people do remember.

Your greatest gift as a clergy leader (and you will not be there to see or hear it) is when someone acts in a way you taught them (by word or example) or says on a particular occasion, "I remember how Chris always used to stress the importance of this." That is leaving a legacy, and it should be your aim as you approach your retirement. This is essentially what I mean when I speak of *pastoral* ministry. And from what I know of you, this has been where you have put the emphasis of your ministry. You will always be glad you did.

Well, this has been a rather long answer to your short question. Yes, I have known people who have turned theory into practice. I have known people who have faced the reality that there has to be a last day and then ordered their words and deeds to make it be as good as they could for themselves and those they serve. I will give thanks to God as long as I live for the witness of David McKenna toward this goal. I hope that I am being that kind of witness now, and I pray that you will be as well where you serve and among those you love.

Blessings!
Steve

A Monastic Experience

Dear Chris,

I am glad what I wrote about David McKenna was helpful to you. Thanks, too, for your kind words about my own attempt to make retirement a holy experience. I have miles to go on many of these things, and I find that my feelings about retirement are not fixed and final. They fluctuate, and yours will too. I accept your invitation to turn from David McKenna to myself, responding to the question, "What is your overarching experience about being retired?"

On one level, it is an impossible question to answer because retirement is a multifaceted experience. But I think the overarching experience is that it has given me the opportunity to be a monk. Given your own interest in historic monasticism and your reading of the new monastics, I imagine you can relate to much of what I am about to write.

As you know, the word *monk* literally means "singular." Rather than describing a particular kind of lifestyle, or a set-apart location, it has more to do with living a life that is focused. The cloistered dimension (ancient and modern) is only a tangible means for providing that focus. As you also know, we misunderstand the monastic life if we believe it is only for monks and nuns. In its essence, it is an experience for every Christian—akin to Jesus's exhortation to abide in him (John 15) and Peter's admonition for Christians to continue to grow in the grace and knowledge of our Lord Jesus Christ (2 Peter 3:18).

So, moving into the early years of retirement has enabled me to become monastic, and to live with increased focus. Honestly, I lived in the world of institutional Christianity for so long that I did not realize how much it scatters us, fragmenting our attentiveness largely into dealing with a diversity of activities that never end. I do not say this critically, for most of the things we give ourselves to as clergy are good things. But what I didn't realize until I retired was how many things there were, and how much I had been living "far and wide" in relation to all the things I had to do.

One of the things I chose to do even before I retired was to re-read *The Rule of Benedict* and about a half dozen books written about it. I am so glad I did. Not only did I reconnect with the spirit of these early monastics, I also came to realize that their basic pattern was doable for me. As you will recall, the Benedictine order (and that of other monastic orders) is twofold: worship and work. Worship is the central act; in fact, it can be seen as a thread that runs through the whole of the day, punctuated by personal (*lectio divina*) and communal (choir) acts of worship. But Benedict knew that an intense and never-ending interiority (such as monasteries and convents call for) could become deformative. So, he brought work into the picture of whole-life Christian formation. And as you will know, this worship/work pattern became the heart of monastic spirituality.

What I have found in retirement is that I can follow the same pattern. Of course, there are daily exceptions, but overall it has been joyous to discover that retirement can be a monastic experience. Jeannie and I have established a worship/work pattern. We use the morning hours for worship—prayer, reading, silence, solitude—and then after lunch, we move into some kind of work, either at home or in the community. So far, this has been delightful for both of us. For one thing, it is a much more restful pace of living, but within that larger sense of sabbath, retirement enables us to be more attentive to whatever it is we are doing in any given moment. Rest is transformed into refreshment. Life is *good*.

Chris, I had lost consciousness of how my present moments were frequently cluttered (perhaps even controlled) by what had happened before the moment, and what was going to happen after it. So, while I was existing in the present moment, I was not always *living* in it. For example, in my years of seminary administration, I would often find myself in a meeting thinking more about the last meeting or the next one than the one I was in at the time! Of course, no one could hear this "collateral noise" going on in my head. But I could, and I often found it to be distractive. Like Martha, I was worried and troubled about many things—sometimes too many.

Retirement does not completely solve the problem, and particularly when we are patterned to keep multiple plates spinning at once. I am, and likely always will be, activistic in my basic temperament. But I must tell you that retirement affords more opportunity to pay attention to the present moment and to do fewer things with greater devotion. For example, if I find in my morning devotion that a passage of scripture has really engaged me, I do not have to give it passing interest; I can continue to sit with it (sometimes even for more than an hour) allowing the initial encounter to become contemplative. There are other ways this happens, but the point is, I now have time as a gift in itself—not something that moves me too quickly from one thing to another.

I hope writing this way brings you to the word *fun*. Retirement provides numerous opportunities to discover enjoyment in ways that running from one thing to another often prevents. Retirement is teaching me that joy abides, not just appears. I can extend the moments of joy, making the overall experience broader as well as deeper. As I do this, I find that particular moments almost always have more than one grace gift in them—again, something I too often missed when I moved from one moment of time to another "naming" it in advance according to its agenda. The result is the paradox of focus, where living in the present moment creates focus.

Growing up in West Texas, I learned something that has stayed with me all my life. During our hot summers, I would sometimes go out into the backyard and gather dry grass and leaves. I would take my magnifying glass and focus the light of the sun onto the little pile I had made. You know the rest of the story. As I increasingly focused the light into a single beam, it ignited the pile into a fire. Even to this day, I am amazed at how light can magke fire.

Chris, it is not an accident that many of our predecessors in the faith (including John Wesley) used the analogy of fire to describe those moments that ignite significant things in us. But as was the case for me with my magnifying glass, the saints of the ages knew that fire follows focus. Of course, we do not have to wait until retirement to experience this, but I can tell you for sure that retirement gives you more opportunities to take the light of God and focus it through your soul, resulting in what one early monk called "becoming all fire."[1]

I hope this exchange of letters is helping you anticipate retirement as a means to having your heart "strangely warmed" as much as any other phase of life you have lived—perhaps even more!

Blessings!
Steve

---

1. Benedicta Ward, trans., *The Sayings of the Desert Fathers* (Kalamazoo: Cistercian Publications, 1975), 103.

Discerning the Time

Dear Chris,

It is time to think about constructing the spiritual house that will exist on the kind of foundation we have laid. We need to spend some time on the general dynamics of a good spiritual house as it pertains to retirement. As Jesus predicted, every house will face strong winds. It needs to be built on a good foundation. So, let's consider this letter as the beginning of a departure from pure theory on the one hand, but prior to innumerable specifics on the other.

For me, there is only one place to begin, and that is by using one word: discernment. When we align ourselves with the pending reality of our retirement, we must ask, "When should I do this?" A retirement that has the kind of spirituality we've described must include asking, seeking, and knocking regarding the timing of it. That's discernment. It is doing our best to find the *kairos* intersection with our *chronos*. I believe that for us clergy, the intersection is made up of two commitments—each of which we have some responsibility for bringing to pass.

The first is the commitment you make to yourself—to retire when the congregation is doing well. That may seem obvious, but I can tell you for sure that some clergy stay on too long; they stay until the momentum they have worked so hard and faithfully to achieve begins to diminish. They stay until one of the largest unspoken questions (at least to the pastor) is, "How much longer is he or she going to be here?"

Whenever I think about this, I remember a conversation that Dr. Thomas Carruth and I had one evening, sitting at the kitchen table of the first church I served after graduation from seminary. Dr. Tom had so influenced me that I wanted to share the blessing of his life and ministry with the folks at First United Methodist Church in Roby, Texas. We invited him to come for a weekend renewal event—one that made a lasting impact on our congregation and the community.

As we were visiting, the topic of clergy moving from one place to another came up. With his usual combination of simplicity and wisdom, Dr. Carruth said, "Well, the only thing I know is this: it is better to move one year too early than one year too late." I'm sure I nodded in agreement, but I can remember not really having any idea what that meant in terms of actually figuring it out. I was too new in the ministry to embrace his words at the level he was speaking them. Years later, I still do not have any formula for determining when that "early year" is occurring. Experience tells me that it is not something we can ever predict with absolute certainty, but I also know that it is something we must use as a means for planning our retirement.

It means deciding to retire when many factors combine to say there really is no need to do so. If we wait to consider retiring when we have to do it, we have waited too long. I have known pastors who did not finish well, because their final years were ones of hanging on while a growing number of folks were hoping they would hang it up. Forced terminations are never pleasant, and they can dull the good work that has been done, like a film on one's tongue that alters the flavor of the food. Chris, you do not want to allow this to happen to you. People have a tendency to remember final things, not things that happened years ago. Determine to make the final memories between you and your people good ones. This approach will not prevent anyone from being sad when the time to die arrives, but sadness is far better than staying until people are more happy to see you leave than wish you would remain.

I had to deal with this as a professor, not as a pastor, but the principle of leaving one year early applied when the time came. For me, it meant not investing myself in new programs that would require me to stay on. On one occasion I had to say that I would not accept a particular responsibility because I did not imagine I would be around long enough to see it through. I was determined not to commit to anything that would make it easy for me to say to myself, "I cannot leave now." In a strange way I knew that to do so would actually end up being my decision, not the decision of the institution I was serving, because (truth be told) I would be the one who engineered the alleged extension.

So, don't do it. Look at the main things that are contributing to the well-being of your congregation and determine to time your retirement in a way that does not attach anything new to what is already there. This does not mean becoming stagnant or unimaginative; it just means handing off the church to your successor with things going as well as you can. It is much easier for the next pastor to work with what is healthy than to have to attempt to revive what is sick. I have known many churches that were set back for years in their liveliness by pastors staying longer than they should have. It is not good for the pastor or the congregation.

The second commitment is the one you make to the congregation—to announce your retirement in plenty of time for them to process their initial sense of sadness and to move into the healthy place of planning well for the transition. I told you about the way

David McKenna dealt with this, and I repeat it now because I think this is especially important when a congregation has had a pastor like you—someone who has been there for a while. Everyone gets comfortable in assuming that the good things will go on forever. Even when you or your people entertain the idea that you will not be there forever, the sense of comfort easily dulls the mind to reality and postpones the transition work.

If you announce your retirement with insufficient time for your people to process it, you will be asking them to make good decisions when they are in a reactive mode, rather than in a responsive mode. This often plays out when people say, "Well, whatever else, we want the next pastor to be like you," when the fact is, the next pastor may need to be different, and when the reality is that the next pastor simply cannot be like you. Reactionary responses—those not given sufficient time to arise and mature—are more likely to produce unreal expectations among your people than planning your retirement in a way that gives them time to deal with their feelings and with the facts that need to be dealt with in order for the church to move ahead in the best possible way.

Chris, you are in an appointive process, not a congregational-call process. But even when the larger judicatory body works to find your successor, it happens best when the leaders in your church have time to really ask and discover where the church is presently strong and weak and where it needs to maintain momentum or gain a new vision. Here is a place where your pastor-parish committee should swing into gear. If you have chosen them well and worked with them effectively, this is precisely the team to do the kind of assessment that they will need to have in hand in order to work with the superintendent to help him or her bring forward a new pastor who is more likely to succeed than fail.

So, it is all about discernment—yours and the congregation's. And it is your call to initiate both aspects of the discernment process.[1] With respect to yourself, you will look back on a decision to leave "one year too early" as born of wisdom; and with respect to your congregation, you will remember the closing time of your pastorate as one when you helped the church build its bridge into the future and then walked with them across it. And although it will never be executed perfectly, you will find it to be a better plan than keeping your plans to yourself and pulling the plug too late for anyone to have time to use your retirement as the occasion for creating a forward look.

Blessings!
Steve

---

1. My book *Walking in the Light* (Nashville: Upper Room Books, 2014) is about discernment. You may find it helpful in expanding some of the ideas in this letter and implementing them in the congregation. Henri Nouwen's writings on discernment have also been compiled into an excellent volume entitled *Discernment* (San Francisco: HarperOne, 2013).

Ready to Retire?

Dear Chris,

There is another question for us to consider as we approach retirement: "How do I know if I am ready to retire?" That is a different question than knowing *when* to retire. I can stick with the analogy of the spiritual house that I offered you in the last letter. Jeannie and I had the opportunity to build a house when we moved to Nashville to become part of the General Board of Discipleship/Upper Room team. I learned a lot from that experience, some of which I found applicable in my deciding to retire.

I found that the decision had to be made on a good foundation. That's why I began our correspondence with spiritual formation principles. I also learned from building a house that the process takes time, and the more patient we can be, the better decisions we make. That's why I am glad you are thinking about retirement now, rather than waiting until you have to compress a host of things into a short timeline. On one level, you may find your anxiety level higher (that is, "Do I have to deal with all this right now?"), but in the long run, you will be glad you did.

With respect to your readiness to retire, I want to focus this letter on some selected external factors. The first is what I would call your personal research. Think of it like putting Velcro on the wall of your life. Once it is there, other things will stick to it. But without it, things you might need to consider can bounce off and go unnoticed and unattended.

Looking back to my own records, I realize that I began this research phase when I decided to become a member of AARP. The small annual membership fee opened the door to a wealth of materials that helped me think about my future retirement, which was still about fifteen years away. In the beginning, I did not study retirement information with great focus and intensity; in fact, some of the stuff they sent me went into the trash. But the fact that they kept sending me materials about retirement had an effect upon me. The materials that arrived in my mailbox kept me thinking about it, and doing so with a lot of tried-and-true information. I created a file to capture material that seemed to fit my life and situation.

The only thing to remember is that any retirement organization is going to be tied to products in some way—either via advertisements or actual things the organization recommends. But if you don't feel pressure to purchase something (at least not now), you will find a host of valuable resources and information. Later on, someone told me that Kiplinger's publishes an annual retirement planning guide. I purchased one in 2008 and another one in 2010 and found the contents to be quite helpful. In all of this, I chose not to write off for "further information," because I did not want to get on mailing lists that could complicate a process I was trying to keep as simple as possible at that stage of the game.

In addition, I found I could always go online and search for both general and specific items about retiring. The point here is simply that one of the best things you can do is to arm yourself with general information about retirement. This will help you move into the second phase of assessing your readiness with some knowledge already in hand, so that you can seek good advice, ask beneficial questions, and so forth. Personal research helps you combine collective wisdom about retirement with your own particular issues related to it.

In this phase of personal research, I also asked others if there was a book about retirement that they had found helpful. Interestingly, I found one recommended more than once, and when I read additional reviews, I felt it was something that would enhance my own study.[1] I began reading it when I stepped down from my administrative position at the seminary—three years before I entered into full-time retirement. Books like this come and go, so you can check out currently available ones. The point is, outlines, charts, bullet points, and short articles are useful, but there are some things that need more depth and substance. The book I selected provided a deeper look at retirement, with additional references and online links to take me even farther if I wanted to do so.

As you engage in this kind of personal work, a second dimension to assessing readiness will merge into your life: the need to have conversations. In fact, I do not know how anyone would retire without including a lot of talk in the process. The topics tend to cluster around personal, physical, relational, and social matters. And as you explore them, you will naturally think of people who can help you with different ones. Foremost in this is your spouse, for no one will journey with you into and beyond retirement in the ways your spouse will. From the moment I began to think about retirement, Jeannie became my best conversation partner and greatest supporter. A lot I am writing about to you has come about because of her wisdom and love. But you will also have others in your church, community, family, and extended friendship network who can be valuable conversation partners.

---

1. Daniel R. Solin, *The Smartest Retirement Book You'll Ever Need* (New York: Penguin Group, 2009).

But the place you will want to begin in assessing your readiness for retirement is with yourself. If you do not start with yourself, you run the risk of later on blaming someone else for your decision. But even more, the clergy I have talked with confess that the main obstacles to retirement were inside themselves, or at least formidable enough to defer dealing with the external factors. Here are some questions other pastors gave me to consider, and I pass them on to you:

- Can I cut back on "work time" and devote less time to professional life?
- What retirement roles can legitimately keep my gifts and graces alive?
- What existing or possible activities have potential to generate some income?
- Do I already have fulfilling non-professional activities?
- What do I want to do alone in retirement? What do I want to do with others?

Questions like these help us to have quiet talks with our own souls, and they can help us create momentum to move outside ourselves to glean encouragement and guidance from others.

The physical dimension to retirement readiness will likely come into play while you are working in the personal domain. With respect to the physical, you can consider these things:

- Are you in good health for your age?
- Do you pay attention to things like diet, exercise, and sleep?
- Are you at or near a proper weight for a person your age?
- Do you know how health insurance works for retirees?

Questions like these help you plan to move into retirement in as good of health as you possibly can. If you have a good primary care physician, readiness to retire might include asking him or her what other factors contribute to a good retirement at the physical level.

With respect to relational factors, I have in mind such things as the way you and your spouse will work out retirement dynamics, as well as members of your family and others who need to play a formative role. You can consider questions like this:

- Will (or should) my spouse continue to work after I retire?

- Can we create separate space at home for each of us?

- How can I foster "life" in my spouse, and my spouse in me?

- How will we share household responsibilities?

- What do we look forward to doing together?

- Do we have a friendship network beyond ourselves?

- How will our family be helpful—or potentially problematic?

- What have we learned from previous life changes that can help us now?

Questions like these can help you arrange and activate the social network that provides a larger context for your retirement.

Regarding social considerations, I have in mind drawing on existing people and resources in your church and community. There are people who help others retire and who can help you make connections you might never think of on your own. You can consider these kinds of questions as you seek to link your retirement to outside assistance:

- Who do I know who seems to have retired well?
- What members do I have that I can turn to for professional advice?
- What local, state, and federal resources are available for retirees?
- Do I have a lawyer with whom to discuss legal matters (e.g., wills)?
- Do I have a financial consultant?
- What resources does my denomination provide to help folks retire well?

You will have to decide whether to explore social resources after you have announced your decision to retire, or if you can begin to do this prior to making a decision and announcing it. I know clergy who have chosen one way over the other, so I am not sure one is better. You know yourself and your situation.

Chris, when you merge the two streams of personal research and conversations, I am confident you will be able to know if you are ready to retire. This kind of exploration creates a sense within us that defines readiness positively and motivates us to begin putting it onto a timeline that inspires us to view the transition as part of God's will and a way to lead us into abundant living apart from the work we have done for so long.

Blessings!
Steve

Announcing the Decision

Dear Chris,

If you discern your readiness to retire, the matter of when to announce your decision is in the wings. As they say, "timing is everything." In considering your timing, remember there are multiple dimensions to the announcement. You will have to announce your decision more than once.

The first announcement is the one you and your spouse will make to each other. As I emphasized at the beginning of our correspondence, retirement is never something you do by yourself. And as a married person, that is even truer for you. Assuming that both you and your spouse have been pondering retirement individually and collectively, you will be moving closer and closer to the shared reality of saying, "The time is at hand." Hopefully, the questions in the last letter will be useful to the two of you, and as you assess your readiness, others will flow naturally into your conversation.

Jeannie and I began to talk of retirement about six years before I actually announced it. As I told you, it began during a sabbatical that we used to travel across the country and back over a period of nearly eight months. The experiences that we had as we did this generated conversations about how good and fun it would be to be able to do this kind of thing more often and that retirement would open a door to being able to do it. These conversations were not an albatross that hung around our necks all that time, but there were occasions that focused our attention on the future. The conversation was both literal and figurative. We talked about our real-life issues that needed to be addressed. And we used the time to begin reading more about the retired life. I began to pay closer attention to what was coming from AARP and other sources.

But what helped most was the growing sense that we were moving forward together by agreeing that the time was drawing near. I cannot speak for Jeannie, but I can tell you that one of the greatest retirement gifts I received was what she has been giving me for more than forty-five years—her unwavering support. Jeannie's "go for it" spirit encouraged me again and again, a spirit that included (as it always has) honest interaction and wise counsel. This ongoing conversation flowed into the announcement we made to each other that retiring was something we both needed and wanted to do. We reached the point holding hands.

The second announcement was to the president of the seminary, Dr. Ellsworth Kalas. As a vice president, I served on his cabinet, so he needed to be one of the first to know what I had decided to do. I used our first occasion together to break the news and begin receiving his counsel relative to my decision. I will be forever grateful for our visit. While he was surprised and a bit saddened to learn what I intended to do, he did not try to talk me out of it. He trusted the discernment process Jeannie and I had been going through, and he offered his confidential support as we worked out further details. The initial announcement to him enriched the remaining time we had together.

Chris, I take this second announcement level to mean that you will eventually want to talk with your supervisors about your plans. One of the things we forget about those who oversee us is that they regularly walk with clergy who are retiring. They have seen retirement go well and not so well. Our supervisors are a deep well of wisdom and support, and by bringing them into our counsel, we will gain insights we would not have had otherwise. Moreover, they need time to discern what they feel will be best for the next chapter in the life of the congregation.

The announcement to your supervisors will also kick into play the important phase of connecting you to the resources your denomination has to offer. The investments you have made into a pension plan will now be interpreted in ways that can help you make good decisions about things like post-retirement investment options. Also, you may be part of a judicatory that has pre-retirement seminars for clergy and their spouses. Jeannie and I attended one such event, and we found it to be helpful. In addition to addressing the financial aspects of retiring, the seminar we attended provided us with other valuable information, and it also put us in fellowship with people who were considering retirement themselves.

The third-level announcement is sharing your decision with a few laity in your congregation. I do not know your situation, but in general I would advise you to do this with only one or two folks whom you know to have your best interests at heart and who (this is essential) have the capacity to maintain confidentiality. You may still be months away from making a public announcement, so you need to do your best to ensure that you can speak openly with the assurance that what you share (and what your folks share with you) will be kept confidential. Everything I know about this level (both by study and experience) tells me that the danger lurking in this multilayered announcement process is the word getting out too soon. If that happens, some people will already begin to treat you like a lame duck. Of course, you cannot absolutely guarantee this will not happen, but you must do your best to ensure that it doesn't. This is not secrecy; it is laying a good foundation with respect to your retirement without tearing down your platform for remaining a spiritual leader in your church.

Chris, the previous paragraph may seem rather dark and foreboding. So, I hasten to say that I believe you have folks in your church who can keep confidence with you. I suspect that some have come to your mind while you are reading this. The fact is, if you choose the right people, they will take it as a compliment that you would bring them into your circle of advisors with respect to this important decision. And, as with your supervisors, you can expect that this small group of friends will have important insights to offer you as you move closer to the time when you actually retire, especially if you draw upon their expertise (e.g., lawyers, insurance agents, financial planners) or glean from their personal experiences. Some of them will walk with you to your last day on the job, and beyond.

A fourth-level announcement is bringing forward the gleanings from the previous three levels and declaring your decision to the group in your church that is responsible for handling pastoral transitions. Again, I cannot give you a formula for this. But generally, I would say that you can do this just before, or just after, you begin your final year of ministry in the congregation. I know pastors who have done it both ways. Either way, I would not do this until your final year is official and not subject to change.

But once it is in place, you can talk about your retirement with those who will both help you make a good ending and who will oversee the new beginning. Here again, you need to urge confidentiality for a while, because there are things to be done in your final year that do not need to be undermined by loss of momentum and interest. This group should help you craft the succession plan, one that serves you and the congregation in a good way. So, it is in everyone's best interests to work on this without having to deal simultaneously with secondary matters and unnecessary detours.

The final announcement you will need to make is the public one to the congregation. David McKenna calls this a "clear, clean, and quick decision."[1] The decision is clear in that you are not leaving yourself open for others to talk you out of it. It is clean in that you can assure your hearers that you and the lay leaders of the congregation have crafted a good succession plan. And it is quick in the sense that you are not dragging this out over an extended period of time or using this as the first of many "good-bye moments."[2] The quickness of the decision is not about rushing it, but rather communicating your sense of anticipation that retirement is a time to live the abundant life in a new way.

Chris, I cannot put this on a timeline for you. You can use your discernment process to frame the conversations you have with your spouse, your supervisors, your small group, the transition committee, and the congregation. The public announcement should come when the most folks are present to hear it. Doing it in the summer preceding your retirement is, for example, not a good time. Nor are Sundays on and around holidays. The public announcement should be made so that as many as possible can hear it "straight from the horse's mouth."[3]

If you are like me, you may be a bit surprised that announcing your decision is a multifaceted thing. But like any journey, the step-

---

1. David McKenna, *The Leader's Legacy* (Newberg, OR: Barclay Press, 2006), 83–89.

2. Unfortunately, I watched a leader use his initial announcement of retirement as the launch of innumerable occasions during his last year of service when he would say, "Well, this is the last time I will ever do this." We conducted his professional funeral multiple times, so many, in fact, that walking with him into retirement was a fatiguing experience for the whole community.

3. If you do it in the context of worship, you might consider using Paul's words in 2 Timothy 4:6-8. The passage has the dynamic of looking backward, but with the "henceforth" anticipation of the future.

by-step experience will itself teach you how to take subsequent steps even better. Announcing your retirement is itself a time to learn and grow even more.

Blessings!
Steve

Facing the Giants

Dear Chris,

I am not surprised that my last letter about announcing your decision to retire has brought you to the place of facing some "giants" that are before you. Inside our spiritual house, we can sometimes feel like "the big bad wolf" is trying to blow it down. But when your house is made out of good bricks, you need not allow concerns to become fears. I do not know of anyone who has retired who did so without having to deal with some big issues, or at least issues that appeared large when they first arose. Let me share some with you that not only I have faced but also fellow pastors have told me they, too, faced.

The one cited most frequently is the "life after retirement" issue. I have referred to it previously, but now is the time to address it in terms of the action we take relative to it. I think the way we deal with this is in our ability to move from the functionality of our role to the vocationality (is that a word?) of it. This transition hinges on our ability to move away from "office" and into "person." For over forty years I was a person holding the office of elder, with the added title of professor accompanying. Without realizing it, clergy like us easily become role defined. We become skillful in the exercise of our office, and that is as it should be.

But all that comes to a crisis point when we consider retiring. Almost from one day to the next, we are no longer the one doing the ministry in a congregation or other setting we've been in for so long. Even our best friends in the congregation look to the next pastor (as they should) for the things they sought from us only days ago. Colleagues, too, put us into a different category, perhaps keeping us on their mailing list but not really expecting us to show up or do much. And to be honest, all this comes as a shock, whether we show it on the outside or not.

So, what's a person to do? The only thing I know to suggest is to cling tightly to the abundant-life conviction and adjust accordingly. What else would we expect but to experience retirement as a strange new world? When we go into a city for the first time, we do not drive as confidently or even accurately as we do on familiar streets. When Jeannie and I are traveling and exploring new territory, she often says, "Slow and steady." That's good advice for the transition into retirement just as much as it is for driving around in a new town. We don't panic, but we do pay special attention. As we do this in retirement, we are likely to find abundant life by driving down two main avenues.

The first one is what I call Similarity Street. Abundant life in retirement is not a brand-new and separate category from your past; it is a new expression of much of what you already do naturally and well. So, stay on Similarity Street and see what is there. Here are a few examples to illustrate what I mean. If you want to continue to preach, tell people. Don't expect them to read your mind. If administering Holy Communion has been a highlight for you, talk with the pastor of the church you begin attending and see if you might join with others in seeing that the sick and shut-in members receive the sacrament regularly. If walking with people into marriage has been something you've really enjoyed, go online and associate with reputable organizations who offer marriage services to people who do not have a clergyperson to help. If guiding folks through grief has been something that has touched your heart, I can almost guarantee you that local funeral homes will have a place for you to serve. And some of my deacon friends tell me that retirement expands their opportunities to link the church and the community through existing service organizations, ending up with deepening their vocation in the world.

In my own case, I have been able to preach, teach, and write—as I have been doing for more than fifty years. The difference—and it is a hugely positive one—is that I can do it on my schedule, rather than someone else's. Retirement moves us into part-time functionality, and that has been one of the greatest blessings and joys for me. I am confident that you will find transferable activities that enable you to continue to use your gifts and graces for the good of others.

Before we leave Similarity Street, let me remind you that almost every charitable organization needs volunteers, or in some cases, even hourly-compensated workers. You can begin by going online to sites like the Retired Senior Volunteer Program, to get a sense of the options that are out there. You can match what you find with agencies in your locale, check out their websites, and then follow up with an actual visit to see if there is something you can do to help. Here is another area where non-clergy skills that you possess can continue to be expressed. Maybe you can coach a local children's sports team, or provide mentoring for young parents, or do minor home repairs for people who don't have the means to pay for service calls. Public schools need all sorts of help during school hours and in after-school programs. And as with your clergy skills, you can set the amount, schedule, and pace for these kinds of involvements.

The previous paragraph leads us onto the second street: New-found Lane, where we can use many of the things I have just written about as means to learn new skills. It's almost impossible to write about this, because the possibilities are so numerous and varied. The point is simply that post-retirement life can be a phase of lifelong learning. Maybe there is something you have always wanted to do. Retirement may be God's timing for it. Every time I go into a Home Depot, there is a list of scheduled "how-to" seminars, and that is only one example of finding life by moving outside our traditional skills and acquiring new ones. My mother did some painting in her older years. Another person I know became something of an expert on the Civil War era. Another person apprenticed with a person who taught him how to repair bicycles. A couple Jeannie and I know took up clown ministry, using it to bring happiness to people in hospitals and nursing homes. Whereas Similarity Street extends the use of existing gifts and graces, Newfound Lane evokes dormant energies, or some we didn't know we had.

Facing the giant of "life after retirement" is a paradox. The truth is, there is *more life* after retirement than before, both in terms of breadth and depth. Our problem is that we falsely equate the part of life we have lived and worked in for so long with "all there is," when the fact is, God places us before more open doors than ever after we retire. To put it simply, the world needs all sorts of help. To use words from the Wesleyan Covenant Prayer, "Christ has many services to be done." The secret is to take initiative—to ask, seek, and knock. And as with so much else in the Christian life, it will be given to us, we will find, and the door will be opened.

Chris, my opening years of retirement have largely been driving on Similarity Street, and I have found much joy and fulfillment continuing things that have shaped me in the past and given my life expression. But as I look ahead, I am beginning to sense a stirring in my soul to see if there is something on Newfound Lane that can bring additional fulfillment. On both streets there is "life after retirement" with many doors standing wide open!

Blessings!
Steve

What Time Is It?

Dear Chris,

Let me turn to another "giant" that others often cite about retirement: time. I do not mean here your sense of time; we have already looked at that. I mean time itself. It is not uncommon to ask, "What am I going to do with all the free time I now have?" The first thing to realize when facing this question is that time is never "free." It is always filled with something. So, the question is not about spending time, but more about stewarding time. This has resulted in a two-dimensional approach—one for the longer haul and one for the living of each day.

For me, longer-haul considerations began by deciding how I actually wanted to live in retirement. Remember, I have not gone far into it yet, so the decision has called for discerning how I want to mix a reasonable continuation of familiar activities with sufficient time to discover new things about life that can only be found in retirement—that is, traveling on both metaphorical streets I wrote you about in the last letter.

In talking with other clergy about this, I find they have achieved what we might call "the calendar blend" of now and later in different ways. Some simply let things happen, and that has worked for them. Others have found ways to force themselves into a mix of ministry and retirement through such things as time shares, scheduled vacations, renting cabins and cottages in places they want to go to, and so forth. So far, Jeannie and I have found our new sense of time through a less-regulated life and through travel.

My plan is a kind of blend of pure spontaneity and reasonable prioritizing. Before I retired, some folks were already saying, "Wow, you will have more time than ever to go to churches to preach and teach." A few opportunities were long-term investments in congregations and church-related institutions. They were all attractive, and they each connected with my sense of vocation and skill set. Early on, I realized that I had to set some boundaries that would give me a place to stand in discerning post-retirement ministry. I did not want to fall prey to what we often hear retirees say, "I've never been busier," as if busyness were some evidence of our ongoing value. I wanted to positively own my identity of "retiree" as I have owned other life-stage designations.

So, if I wanted to be retired, I had to act like it. I have no idea what this will mean as time goes by, but for now it means roughly dividing my time between ongoing ministry activity and a simple non-scheduled approach to life. So far, this means viewing November through March as months to consider ministry invitations, and April through October as retirement living. As you can see, this concentrates most of my ministry engagements after the first of the year through Lent, and so far that has seemed to work well. The months of April through October are good ones for traveling and otherwise enjoying life in good weather. From November through March, I can receive and decide about ministry-related activities.

Clearly, this is not a hard-and-fast plan. But it is one that helps me receive each invitation with perspective and prior thinking. It enables me to say to people, "I am sorry, but I am not available during that time to do what you are asking me to do." Yes, it has meant turning down some things I would have accepted before retirement. But as I have already told you, I don't want to live exactly like I used to.

One other dimension to this scheme is that it allows for local commitments. For example, Jeannie and I generally schedule the third Monday of the month to help serve lunch at a local service center. Putting things like this on the calendar over the entire twelve-month period provide us with a better sense of time, especially in the stay-at-home months. Additionally, we can look at local events (like concerts and plays) during the November through March period and write them into the calendar as well. Finally, the stay-at-home months make it possible for me to fill in for a pastor in town who needs to be away, if doing so does not disrupt other plans.

Chris, I have already violated this plan in my opening years of retirement. No plan works all the time, and I still face temptations to say yes when I should say no. But what I have described above has been a good way to look at my time and not simply assume that every day in the year is "available" to the same extent that every other one is. For me, it is an application of Psalm 90:12—the need to "number our days" so that we can have a wise heart.

Chris, you must come up with your own plan. But I wanted to use my real-life example to show you that it is possible. I am sure the one I have chosen for myself will undergo revision as I learn more and experience more in retirement. The spiritual-formation principle I want to preserve, through whatever plan I adopt, is one I learned from Dallas Willard—that the soul needs the rhythm of engagement and abstinence.[1] I tried to find that in my pre-retirement life, but both because of my activistic temperament and my professional duties, I know that I got out of the pattern more than I either remember

---

1. Dallas Willard, *The Spirit of the Disciplines* (San Francisco: HarperCollins, 1988).

or like to admit. But in retirement, I can return to the pattern and use it to decide how I want to live.

Before I retired, I used to talk about "scheduling my time," but the reality was that too often, time scheduled me! Weeks or months in advance I knew when I was going to teach, where I was going to preach, and what meetings I was expected to attend. It is only as I have retired that I have discovered that I really can schedule my time. That makes it more challenging than simply filling in the calendar with predetermined activities, but it also means that I can step back and look at the formative rhythm and use it to create a bigger picture for living.

Chris, combining what I wrote to you in the last letter—that there is life after retirement—with what I have said in this one, I want to encourage you to think about a way to turn a conviction into a reality. I think I would put it this way: whatever you decide to do with your time, do it as a retired person, not as someone who essentially continues the same pace and program only using the word *retirement* to hide the fact that nothing has really changed.

Blessings!
Steve

Show Me the Money!

Dear Chris,

I am not surprised to learn that our correspondence about time has made you think about money. It's obvious, isn't it? The longer we hope to live in retirement, the more we need to be reasonably assured that we have enough money to see us through those years. In naming money as one of your "giants," you have identified the number one concern of retirees in general. It is not easy to get our minds around the idea of having money when we stop making money. And if you and your spouse are like Jeannie and me, we have essentially lived our lives with the resources coming to us in regular paychecks. The realization that those will stop coming (at least from previous sources) takes some getting used to. At least it did for me.

But you can do it! I think the place to begin is to make your financial decisions in the context of normalcy. All of us can imagine a doomsday scenario in which none of us could survive. But if that happens, things will kick into gear that we cannot predict. And besides, we would not be the only ones experiencing the crisis. If you try to execute a financial plan based on a worst-case scenario, you will probably talk yourself out of retiring. The place to begin is to assume that the financial pillars that have held up your house will continue to do so.

When you get this mind-set, secure a good financial planner. We were fortunate to have one recommended to us by friends with whom we attended seminary decades ago—someone they had been using to guide their financial journey for a long while. And sure enough, he has provided just what we need. I almost feel like stopping here, for if you get a financial planner who is professional and personable, nearly all of your questions can be answered and many of your anxieties alleviated.

I would encourage you to ask your friends if they have found a good financial planner. The more personal you can make this, the better. We did not know the person who became our planner, but the fact that we could tell him that one of his long-time clients had recommended him made things positive from the outset. You may have people in your community or in the community where you intend to live who can either recommend a planner or be one for you.

You can go online and find out who the certified financial planners are in your area, but I found that going online didn't help that much. Everyone listed says they help you! It was much better to be able to walk into an office and say, "We were referred to you by _____and _____." There are people near you who are helping folks retire every day, developing retirement plans for them, and giving other wise counsel.

Here are some things to consider as you determine the planner best suited for you. Find out the type and range of services he or she provides, and match them with the ones you need. Determine the professional licenses that the planner holds. Ask for references, even if you do not plan to actually contact them. Find out how your planner is paid. Some charge flat fees, while others receive commissions related to the financial products you end up selecting. There does not seem to be a general consensus on which payment structure is preferable; it is more about the credentials, qualifications, and overall reputation of the person. Good and honest planners will not take advantage of you.

I think an important factor to consider is how much experience the financial planner has in working out plans for people like you. Our planner has focused for thirty years on public school teachers and the retirement portfolios for them. We clergy have a lot of financial similarities. I didn't want to be guided by someone who dealt with multimillionaires and helped them figure out how to purchase homes in the Rockies and on the Riviera. Our planner does have some large account holders, but the majority are folks like us. Learning that increased my confidence that he could understand us and make realistic recommendations.

Another benefit from our planner has been his ability to connect us with other service providers. He has a person on his staff to help clients deal with social security, Medicare, and health insurance matters. And he was able to refer us to a person who showed us how refinancing our home mortgage could save us several hundred dollars each month. I have confidence you can find a similar financial planner. Ask around.

One final word: when you come down to the time when you are almost ready to "sign on the dotted line" with respect to the actual relationship you will have with your planner, be sure that he or she gives you a summary of your financial plan, with estimates as to what each part of it will provide to you. I found that individual contracts were lengthy and detailed (even though I did my best to read through them); what I needed to see before everything became official was an overview of the plan and its initial provisions. I still remember the meeting when my advisor said, "I think you and

Jeannie are in a position to retire." Hearing those words enabled me to cross the line and begin to put things on an actual timeline.

As you search for your financial planner, get organized. Update your family budget, so you can tell accurately what you are spending month-to-month right now. Don't worry a lot about trying to figure out where you might cut back in retirement. Your financial advisor can help you work on things like that, including the possibility that some things might increase. What you need at the start is a good snapshot of your income/expense current reality.

Also, gather information about your social security payment estimates, potential income from pension plans, current balances in your bank accounts, and any other investments you have that will generate future income. Gather similar information about your spouse as applicable. To this information also gather mortgage and escrow data, insurance policies, and the past several years of tax records. And while you are at it, update your wills, beneficiary designations, powers of attorney for health care and financial matters, living wills, and other legal documents that will either have an immediate or eventual impact on your life.

As you do this, envision the financial goals you want to establish in retirement. An income stream sufficient for your anticipated years in retirement is one goal. But you also want to think about elective options that can take you beyond the basics now and then, or perhaps on some kind of regular basis. For retirees, this is often summed up in the word *travel*. Funds to "see the world" and "visit the kids" need to be factored into the plan. You may have other outside-the-budget considerations that need to be factored into the picture.

Bring this kind of information with you to your first meeting with your chosen advisor. Add to that some wet-clay estimate of what your cash flow will look like in retirement. You will be able to calculate this using the distribution amounts that will come from pension plans, the income you will receive from social security, investment income payouts, and any personal income you can reasonably expect to generate. In my case, the calculation was not difficult, because our finances are not complicated. We derived monthly income from five streams: two social security incomes, two pension plans, and one investment account.

On the expense side, we were told by almost everyone that we would not spend as much in retirement as we were spending in current living. Honestly, I was skeptical. But it has turned out to be the truth. Of course, we could spend in ways that would equal or exceed what we were making before retirement, but I am referring now to the continued lifestyle we have grown accustomed to over the years, and for us at least, we do not spend as much each month as we used to. So, it is likely that what the advisors say is true—a monthly income of about 80 percent of what you were making will likely be sufficient. Again, here is where your financial planner can look at your total assets and give you a model that works for you. Economic times fluctuate. There are decisions you can make that can interface current reality with contingencies.

Generally speaking, our cost of living goes up in future years, but our basic expenses go down as we reduce our activities. I am not far enough into retirement to have a sense of this in detail. Nothing has changed dramatically or in a way that ongoing conversations with our financial planner could not either anticipate or handle. The mistake is to think we are at the mercy of increasing costs, but we forget that as time goes by, we can make decisions that have the potential to reduce expenses and increase income. Also, some of your income streams will provide modest annual increases. So far, all this has kept our initial financial security intact.

My initial visits with my financial planner taught me to create a financial plan that has diversity in it, so that as factors in the market change, the entire ship rides out the waves. So, some of our money is in an LTIH (long-term investment hedge fund) that not only helps us know future living expenses can be absorbed but also makes available funds for things such as special vacations or home repairs. Some of our money is invested by the original pension holders—in our case the denomination and the educational pension plan company that managed most of our money since 1970. These funds are essentially fixed, but one has yielded small annual increases. Social security income has also shown small annual increases.

Related to the financial plan itself was our decision to continue the home-equity loan we had taken out previously. These can be renewed for ten-year periods. We are in our second period. And because the equity in our home has become substantial, holding the home-equity loan gives us an ability to use funds for maintenance and other things at one of the lowest-possible interest rates. Maybe you already have a home-equity loan. If not, I would encourage you to consider it.

This brings up the question of a reverse mortgage. They are advertised all over the place these days. My research landed me on the hesitant side. This is certainly something to discuss with your financial advisor and with others you know (like bankers, lawyers, insurance agents) who will have had the opportunity to see the potentials and pitfalls of this kind of fund. Reverse mortgages may work for some, but they are not the "cure all" option they appear to be in the advertisements. They come with liabilities and risks you may not want to incur. Because our homes are the largest investment we have, it is only wise and prudent to be careful about how we commit them to legal obligations in the future.

In addition to making decisions about money itself, you will want to make decisions that provide lifetime payment options and spousal survival security. This will likely mean receiving an initial smaller monthly amount from some accounts, but it ensures that you and your spouse will receive the agreed-upon amounts as long as either of you lives. You do not have to invest this way, but Jeannie and I decided to take a bit less now, so we have guaranteed income for life. In our case, the lesser amount was not as important as knowing that the initial arrangements would be in force until we both die.

Finally, talk with representatives of your denominational pension plan and any other plan holders. Your financial planner may not be as expert in clergy retirement as he or she is about other types. In my case, my financial planner wanted to visit by phone with these representatives during the planning process (which has to be in your presence and with your permission), but it was good to have some preliminary data and contact information in hand for the planner to use.

As I mentioned, quite a bit of our denominational information came by attending a pre-retirement seminar sponsored by our Annual Conference. Check to see if your judicatory provides this. Denominational pension representatives were present with access to my service record. Other professionals made presentations on things like making wise investments, having a will, considering long-term health care, and so on. A panel of recent retirees spoke about some of the real-life issues related to retirement. If nothing else, that seminar got Jeannie and me into the psychological and practical ballpark necessary for us to continue playing the retirement-planning game.

In addition to what your denomination provides, you may also discover that local educational institutions offer courses and seminars for people approaching retirement. For example, one of our local colleges offers one entitled "Retirement Planning Today." For a small tuition fee, it is available to people between the ages of fifty and seventy. Publicity for the course showed that it offered information about eight retirement-related activities. We did not enroll because the course was offered after we had already dealt with the eight items. But had that not been the case, it is good to know that this means of assistance was there.

The main thing to realize is that financial planning is not something you do once during the retirement process. It is something you continue to do all along the way. Financial planners call it "rebalancing" your portfolio. It has largely to do with gaining an increased wisdom about your expenses (via your growing years of experience), updated information about your income (via new decisions about how best to leverage what you have), and blending that with new financial goods and services that may enhance your overall financial strength.

Chris, I am going to end this letter where I began it—with the counsel to get a good financial planner and let that person begin mapping your retirement. And a map is what it is—to navigate what we all hope will be a journey that lasts between twenty and thirty years. I am amazed that more than three years is already behind us. The advice we originally received from our financial advisor has been good, and the implementation of that advice, combined with the same good money-management practices Jeannie and I have used for more than forty-five years, has provided us with a good platform for enjoying our retirement without having to worry about money.

Blessings!
Steve

Home, Sweet Home!

Dear Chris,

You're absolutely right! There is a direct connection between money and housing. As I said in the last letter, your home can be a source of funds. But it is also likely to be the single-greatest place for spending money as your house ages. Housing considerations are major factors in everyone's retirement, but especially so for clergy.

You are living in an unfurnished parsonage, so I will orient this letter around that reality. But you said that you have friends in other kinds of housing situations who have asked you about this topic, so I will do my best to suggest options that you might find useful as you share with them.

First and foremost, don't forget that your clergy housing allowance continues to apply in retirement. As long as you (as the ordained person) are alive, it remains in effect. So, this will continue to be a valuable tax deduction in the future. The most helpful guidance about this for me came through denominational information. I think it is good to know how the clergy housing allowance is viewed by those who are closest to your ecclesial reality. I took what the denomination had to offer and compared it online with other denominations. There was not a lot of variation, and in one case, I found a helpful form to use in calculating each year's deductions and whether or not to take the Fair Rental Value option or go the Actual Expense route.

I took this information to my financial advisor to integrate into the plan he was developing. He welcomed the information, verified it, and used it to further develop our retirement plan. You will notice above that I pointed out that if the ordained person dies, the clergy allowance goes away. That was good for our financial advisor to know, because it is a loss that needs to be in view. Of course, the cost of living for your spouse will be less, but the difference between losing the allowance and lessening the expenses may not even out. In terms of our plan, the potential for losing the housing allowance affected how much we wanted to invest in the LTIH part of our funds. We are reasonably sure that the loss of the clergy housing allowance will not adversely affect Jeannie's financial existence. And as we have learned from other clergy spouses, she may not even choose to remain in the same house—which puts the whole matter back on the table for review later on.

As important as this is, it only looks at the housing issue from a financial and tax standpoint. There are other things to consider. So, let's return to your particular situation. You have been in your parsonage for nearly seven years, and by the time you retire, it could be closer to ten. One option that some clergy are using these days is to ask if the church would be willing to sell the parsonage to them and use the proceeds to buy another one elsewhere in the community. You will know whether or not this is something you should consider; I just want you to know that it is a workable scenario in some places—one that could virtually eliminate your need to move, allow you to continue to make your home "yours" as it has become over the years, and at the same time allow the church to upgrade their official parsonage with a new house in another location.

Along with this option, however, I would say that an even larger factor for you could be how close and involved you want to be after you retire. To be honest, I am not sure I would act on this option, because my view is to cast no shadows on the church and your successor. Even if you stay in the same community, you may want to establish your retirement home in another part of town. But again, I trust you can discern what is best.

If you do choose to move, carefully consider the location. Here I do not mean another part of town (although that would surely be a location issue too), but rather whether or not your transition into retirement would be better served in a completely new location. To be sure, this is a more radical decision, but it may be one that you would find more practical and enjoyable. Here is where research is once again in order. Find out how favorable your option is for retirees in general, and then check to see if the goods and services you will need are available in the new place. Also, see if the recreational features of a new location fit your interests. You can get this kind of information online by researching each possible city or area.

If your new location is closer to one child than another, you want to be sure you avoid the "favored child" appearance. The best way to do this is to have everyone involved in the decision-making process, while making it clear that you and your spouse will be the ones to decide where to live, and that wherever you end up living is for your benefit, not theirs. Hopefully, your children will be able to celebrate your choice without factoring their secondary issues into the picture. Conversation is the best way for this to happen positively.

No matter where you decide to live after you retire, the new location will be challenging because it will distance you from friends you may have become close to. But if they are parishioners, that is probably a good thing. You are not their pastor after you retire;

hanging out together can make the break harder to achieve. But here is where clergy may have a leg up on laity. You have grown accustomed to moving over the years, having to form new friendships in each place. So hopefully, the thought of doing it again will not be an impossible thing to consider. And if there is somewhere you have talked about living when you retire, it could be a positive factor as you look forward to being in that place.

In talking with clergy who have relocated, some tell me that they found it good to rent at first. Unless you move into a rent-to-buy house, it does mean having to move again. But folks who have done this tell me that by living in the new community for a while, they were able to make a better long-term housing choice. We have never done this exactly as you may do it in retirement, but when we moved to Nashville, the move included building a new house. We lived in a small furnished apartment for about seven months. The moving company was able to store our belongings during that period, so when we finally moved into our new house, it did not feel like a complete second move. We had only kept out the bare essentials for living in the apartment.

If you do decide to relocate, your decision should include the type of home you want to move into. Do you want to have to take care of a large yard? Do you need some space for a garden or other outside amenity, like a pool or patio area? Do you want to climb stairs or purchase a one-story house? Are you ready to connect with a housing choice that provides you with initial independent living but can be altered at a later time for assistance and care? Of course, you are not locked in to the first choice you make. But if you can get some sense of the type of housing that best suits you, it will likely mean living longer in the house you first purchase.

One final thought may be helpful. When you begin to narrow your options, ask if your home will be under the oversight of a neighborhood housing association. If it is, ask to see the terms and conditions that you will move into. We are fortunate to live in an association where the annual dues are low and the requirements are comparatively few. But that is not always the case. We have some friends who have felt overly scrutinized by the neighborhood association where they chose to live. This consideration falls into the "better safe than sorry" category.

Chris, I hope these comments have been helpful. My situation is far different, because since 1977, we have not lived in a parsonage or had a housing allowance provided to us by a church. Our several moves since then have been in the context of finding a new home, selling our existing one, and moving into the new location. And when I retired, we were able to stay in our existing home—which is far enough away from where I worked so as not to cast the shadow I was telling you to avoid casting.

But even with these differences, I think some of what I have shared will be good for you and your clergy friends to think about. For those who will retire in a home of their own paid for (at least in part) by a housing allowance, it may not be as difficult to figure out these things. After all, they are already in their home, and they can choose to stay in it. Those I worry about the most are clergy who have lived in parsonages most of their career and come to retirement trying to figure out how to suddenly become a home owner. This is where clergy should ask friends who have retired from similar situations, and where they should also seek out denominational and community counselors who can help them enter the "strange new world" of home ownership in the best ways.

There are all sorts of financing options today, but the thing your friends need to be careful about is not putting themselves in jeopardy of foreclosure. Tell them to talk to real estate agents, bankers, and lawyers in their church to begin getting their minds around this. And as you are able, encourage younger clergy to set aside some funds over the years for use when they retire, at least an amount that will cover an average amount expected to be paid at closing—an amount that will be a certain percentage of the selling price, plus closing costs. Not doing this could adversely affect their ability to make the leap into owning a home, if that is what they hope to do when they retire. Again, there are people in their churches who can guide them.

The good news is that we are a mobile society. This has changed the mind-set of those of us who move around, but it has also increased the professional counsel we can receive for making a good move. Here is another place where taking your time and moving slowly will likely pay off. No matter what you plan to do about housing, you want—as much as possible—to live in your retirement home saying, "Home, sweet home!"

Blessings!
Steve

In Good Health

Dear Chris,

You are correct in connecting housing choices with health-care matters. Unfortunately, there is nothing currently so much in flux in the United States as our health-care system. The fluctuations run the gamut of hospitals, insurance plans, physicians, and so forth. Jeannie and I were fortunate to move to Florida and secure the services of a good general practitioner, but she suddenly decided to cease her practice, and we were not prepared for the complexities related to finding another doctor. Advertisements make it appear that doctors are out there just waiting for you to contact them and begin receiving their services. But we have found that there is a lot more to it than that. Each physician has conditions that potential patients must meet in order to be accepted.

If you stay in the place where you are currently serving, you can continue to use the physicians and health-care services you've grown accustomed to. But even if that is the case, I would visit with your doctors to find out how long they plan to keep their practice open and what their general counsel would be for you as you move into retirement. Our doctor was about ten years younger than we are, so we did not expect her to close her practice as quickly as she did. So, I would encourage you to have conversations with your doctors, even if it looks on the surface as though nothing is going to change. And if you are going to relocate, ask your physician for any recommendations of doctors in your new location. Physicians will often accept patients more easily when they are recommended by another doctor.

With respect to health insurance in retirement, here is another item to put on your list to discuss with your financial advisor, denominational officials, insurance agents, and the like. Because our financial planner provides health-care services, we have been spared having to go online and try to figure it out. But those who have done so tell me it is a maze. And for all retirees, there is the annual enrollment period in which you consider whether or not to continue or change whatever health insurance you have. Even though we are only a few years into retirement, we have not come to a renewal period without learning about options that were not available a year ago, and having to decide whether or not to include them in our coverage for the coming year.

Also, we have found that doctors may accept one insurance plan this year but not the next. Be sure to ask your doctor each year if he or she will continue to accept the plan you currently have. But even if he or she will, you may still want to examine other plans to see if any have made improvements you can benefit from. All this is a moving target.

At the same time, this is not hopelessly complex. When you retire at sixty-five or over, you and/or your spouse will be eligible for Medicare. I cringed just thinking about trying to deal with government bureaucracy, but when the time came to actually do so, I found it to be far easier than I ever thought it would be. Even the 800-number for Medicare enrollment was simple to use, and the person I ended up talking with not only was helpful during that first phone call but also continued to serve as a contact as the process unfolded. And even more, when Jeannie approached her sixty-fifth birthday, she got a notice in the mail that she was enrolled automatically, and the packet contained her Medicare card.

In the process of enrolling, I learned that Medicare Part C was an option that essentially provided us with private-carrier health insurance at no cost. At first, I thought this was too good to be true, but the health advisor at our financial planning office helped me understand how it works. When you choose a health insurance company, it is connected with Medicare, and the monthly Medicare premium deduction is paid to the insurance company—with no additional payment asked of you.[1] The only other step was to be sure that our doctor accepted the health plan we were choosing. With the monthly Medicare premium connected to the insurer, and with the coverage that fit our situation and was accepted by our physician, we have been good to go so far.[2] The annual review/decision process has turned out to be good for us, because it gives us the opportunity to update our health-care needs and plan accordingly.

In terms of the timeline, you should discuss this with your physician early each fall, before you have to enroll for a new year of coverage. The enrollment period begins October 15 and runs into early December. If your doctor is going to continue to see you, there will likely be nothing you have to do with Medicare or the private insurance connected with it, since no action on your part automatically continues the coverage you currently have. If you do need to make some changes, your doctor can tell you what you need to know, so that when you meet with your health-care counselor for the annual review of your coverage you can make the right change.

---

1. Not every Part C plan is fully funded by the Medicare monthly deduction. It depends on the carrier and the benefits you want to receive in the plan.

2. Depending on the plan you choose, Part C coverage includes some additional benefits (e.g., vision care), and it also covers medications as Medicare Part D is designed to do if you do not have a Part C plan.

Chris, the only other thing that comes to mind about health insurance is that given that your spouse is younger than you, until she reaches age sixty-five, she will either need to continue her coverage through a COBRA plan that your denomination may allow for or have to secure private-carrier health insurance. Check with your denominational office to see if COBRA is available, and then compare it with the monthly premiums you would pay a private company.

Chris, all of this is predicated on my hope and prayer that you and your spouse will "live long and prosper." Hopefully, the health-care decisions you make in retirement will include the maintenance of a healthy lifestyle with respect to diet, exercise, sleep, recreation, and so on. The thing I like most about my health insurance so far is how rarely I have to use it!

Blessings!
Steve

One of These Days

Dear Chris,

Thanks for asking me to say more about long-term health care. I did not know it was something you feel the need to be better informed about. Jeannie and I have not gone far down the road of exploration, so what I have to say will be limited. But during my personal research phase in pre-retirement planning, I looked into it.

The immediate fork in the road is whether you want to plan for in-home care or for care in another facility. You can get policies that focus on one or the other, and some that combine planning for a transition from in-home care to institutional care. No matter how you go, LTC plans are expensive because the nature of care provided is costly.

Here again, I would urge you to discuss this with your financial planner. He or she will likely be able to provide you with information that will help you make good decisions or guide you to others who can help. Generally speaking, health insurance does not cover long-term care. Medicare provides limited assistance, and Medicaid funds (if you are eligible) provide care only when most of your personal assets have been spent. There are variables to all of this, and that is why I suggest you start with your financial advisor and others who work with long-term care issues daily. One thing you can do is visit with the manager of an assisted-living facility or nursing home the next time you visit parishioners there. You will likely leave that visit with some good advice.

Whether we like to face it or not, data shows that about 70 percent of us will need some kind of long-term care, and 40 percent spend some time in a nursing home. This comes from the natural effects of aging, but it can also arise due to things beyond our control: accidents, prolonged illnesses, and other disabilities. One way to think about it is by asking yourself questions like: If we became sick or disabled tomorrow, who would care for us? How would we pay for the care?

Here is another area where you will likely want to talk with your children, not to put them on the spot, but because when the time comes for needing long-term care, you need to have some basics in mind—and for some, care from family members is one piece of the picture. Also, you need to calculate costs. Right now, for example, Jeannie and I would have enough for either of us to receive long-term care. And if for some reason we needed it together, we could use the LTIH fund to provide it. Remember, the average need is not lengthy, usually only several years. You can develop a long-term care policy that has a particular payout schedule, and it appears that most people choose a three- to five-year coverage period. Further good news is that your LTC policy only needs to cover the gap between what your current income provides and what the care costs. You are not starting from zero.

Perhaps you can tell from what I have written that we do not have a long-term care policy. One thing we did not know when we applied was that pre-existing conditions can cause you to be turned down, or the premiums for care (with or without such conditions) can be beyond reach. That turned out to be the case for us. Even though our current health is good, past circumstances ruled both of us out—at least in terms of what we could afford to pay. So, it is unclear whether we will ever be able to have coverage for long-term care beyond our current resources, other potential assistance, and help from family. Once again, your financial advisor can guide you. These plans change over time like everything else.

Chris, that's the best overview I can give you based on my actual experience. So many companies offer long-term care, and the provisions (some fixed, and some based on your choices) are so varied that to go further would almost certainly be to miss something you may need in your particular situation. I think my singular counsel is that if you are in good health, go ahead and explore the option and see what you can get. The younger you are, the less likely you will be turned down due to health-related problems. And the younger you are, the lower your premiums will be. You do not have to wait until you retire to purchase an LTC policy. I am confident your financial advisor can give you what you need to make a good decision.

Blessings!
Steve

Cared For by Uncle Sam Each Month

Dear Chris,

We are fortunate to live in a country where the government cares for retirees. I am happy to write more about this. I have already written about the basics related to becoming part of Medicare. I will focus now on social security, since both you and your spouse have been paying into it over the years. I know there are clergy who have not done this, and I respect them for their decision. But now that I am retired, I am glad I did. From a purely financial standpoint, about half of our monthly income comes from social security. Retirement would have been much more challenging if we had not been paying into the social security program.

Personally, I do not feel it goes against Christian principles to pay into the social security program and receive benefits from it during your retirement years. Your service to God has included a betterment of the country, and the nation is willing to afford its clergy financial benefits for having done this. Moreover, you have been paying over the years at the self-employment rate, and that can mean larger monthly payments when you retire.

The main thing to do is to give yourself time to familiarize yourself with both the social security and Medicare components of your anticipated benefits from the government. The Social Security Administration provides helpful booklets on both programs. There are also helpful resources available through retirement organizations, in bookstores, and online. What you request from the Social Security Administration can provide the core of your study, and you can branch out from there to get more details on specifics that may apply particularly to you. You may have also been receiving periodic estimates from the government as to what your monthly social security income would be. These few information sources were enough to make a reasonable retirement plan. If you call the social security number, you can talk personally with a customer service representative, who may turn out to be an ongoing contact person as you navigate the process.

Your first decision will likely be when to begin receiving benefits. All the literature states the obvious: the longer you wait to draw payments, the larger each month's payment will be. There is nothing magic here; it's the simple math of deferring compensation. And when you look at the charts, the larger monthly amount at seventy may look like it's worth waiting for. But there are other factors to consider. The annual increases we have received in our first few years in retirement are helping make up the difference in what the age-seventy amount was predicted to be. For us, the overall better plan was to go ahead and begin receiving social security payments at age sixty-five. Jeannie even decided to receive hers before sixty-five, so that her monthly payment could positively influence our monthly income. That does not detract from the fact that waiting longer means a higher monthly check, but it does mean that it is not a decision everyone should make.

One factor to consider is how much you estimate making in retirement. Social security payments can be taxed if your personal income exceeds a certain amount. Each year, I use a form provided by the IRS to see if any of my social security income is taxable. So far, the small amount that is taxable has not outweighed the benefits in going ahead and getting the monthly payment. That is due largely to the fact that the Clergy Housing Allowance deduction offsets any initial downside to receiving social security before age seventy. We pay some for social security, but end up paying less overall because of the housing-allowance deduction we can apply against ministerial services and pension income.

Your financial advisor can gather all the relevant facts about your life and help you determine whether or not to begin drawing social security payments immediately or wait to do so. For example, I know a clergyperson who planned to continue to work part-time in retirement and his anticipated income was high enough for him not to need to receive a social security check immediately. Another clergyperson decided that he could benefit most by receiving benefits at age sixty-two and putting the money into an investment fund that would enable him to purchase a home when he retired. Still another clergyperson chose to begin receiving social security at age sixty-two, and then used the additional income to pay off his mortgage by the time he retired. These are just three examples of the fact that the decision about when to begin receiving benefits varies from person to person.

Whatever you decide to do, the Social Security Administration advises people to apply three months before they want their benefits to begin. To do this, you will need your social security number, your birth certificate, your tax returns for the last year, any military discharge papers (if you served), and the name of your bank and the account where payments will be directly deposited. When you call in (or go online) to begin the process, you will receive precise enrollment instructions.

Let me turn back to Medicare for a moment. If you decide to withhold receiving social security payments until after age sixty-five, you must enroll in the Medicare program close to your sixty-fifth birthday. If you put off enrolling in Medicare until you are over sixty-five, it will likely include some costs for delaying doing so, and there is no need to pay extra for waiting longer. So, be sure you and your spouse enroll in Medicare close to your sixty-fifth birthdays. If you are already enrolled in social security, your entry into Medicare is automatic. But even so, be sure to pay attention to the several months before you turn sixty-five, to make sure it has happened. My enrollment for both social security and Medicare was simultaneous because everything started when I turned sixty-five. Jeannie's choice to receive social security before she turned sixty-five meant that her Medicare enrollment was automatic, since she was already in the social security program. She received notification of her upcoming enrollment (beginning the month she turned sixty-five) about three months prior.

One other helpful thing I learned in applying for social security is that Jeannie will be eligible to continue receiving benefits paid to me if I die before she does, and vice versa. The government recognizes that couples have shared life over all the years, so when one spouse dies, the other can continue to receive the benefits earned by the other—sometimes 100 percent of the spouse's benefits, depending upon the circumstances. Here is another area where specifics vary, so there is nothing more I can say except to remind you that a spouse's benefits do not disappear when he or she dies, but may continue to be paid in some fashion to the surviving spouse.

The only other basic piece that you may find helpful is knowing that your payments will be assigned to the second, third, or fourth Wednesday of the month depending on the day of your birth. The obvious reason for spreading out payments is that it keeps the banking system from crashing, which would happen if all the payment checks hit it on the same day. I tell you this only because you may have to figure your monthly budget a bit differently if your payment date is different from your current payment date. Jeannie and I eliminated that problem by keeping a higher base balance in our account, so that deductions (e.g., mortgage payment) early in the month did not put our account below zero before the social security check—and other income streams that do not pay on the first day of the month—were deposited. If you do something like this, it really doesn't matter when your various retirement payments come into your account.

Chris, there are details beyond this basic information. But not all of them apply to any particular person. So, I would simply advise you to begin doing your homework and interfacing what you find with the conversations you will be having with your financial advisor. If your experience is akin to mine, it will be easier than you might have first thought and the income provided to you by the government for your years of service will be a major plank in your retirement platform.

Blessings!
Steve

Leaving a Precious Gift

Dear Chris,

You raise an important distinction between the economics of a financial plan and those of an estate plan. The kinds of financial considerations we have been exploring have to do with living well in your retirement years. An estate plan is that part of your economic portfolio that deals with how your remaining assets will be passed on after you die. I am happy to tell you what I know about this. Mainly, I see it as an opportunity to leave a precious gift to your heirs.

Over the years, lawyer friends have told me (and I have sometimes observed) that families who have seemed to fare well together in life, do not do so when death comes to one of the family members. Sometimes, the fractures are formidable, prolonged, and permanent. Often this is due to insufficient estate planning on the part of the deceased person, insufficiencies that give rise to various interpretations of the deceased's wishes and the way inheritances were intended to be transferred. This is why I have called estate planning a precious gift. It can clarify and contribute to the transfer of assets from one generation to another. You are wise to be thinking about it.

A lot of your estate planning can be discussed as you make your post-retirement financial plan. Matters having to do with beneficiaries, for example, are required in order to execute investment documents. Jeannie's and my financial life is pretty simple, so in our wills we have made each other the primary beneficiaries of our holdings, with our two children as the next tier of recipients. These designations have been entered into retirement documents as need be.

In addition to this, I think there are some other things to remember about estate planning. One of them is to plan so that your spouse can have sufficient income to live on until all the transfers of funds have occurred. We have done this largely through having enough money in a savings account, and also by keeping a higher balance in the checking account. Some couples set up a separate interest-bearing account to place funds for a spouse to live on for a while, to pay funeral expenses, and so forth. However you choose to do it, be sure to arrange things so your spouse is not "cash poor" and "investment rich" immediately after you die.

Apart from seeking counsel from your financial planner and lawyer friends, there are several other things worth mentioning briefly. Arrange your estate so that maximum privacy is ensured in what is otherwise a matter of public record. There are ways to blend the public domain with things you don't want others to know about. Also, draw up documents in ways that reduce taxes and other expenses related to the settling of your estate. Finally, the estate-planning phase of retirement is a good time to review or establish your philanthropic intentions. You may have done this in your will, but even so it is timely to be sure that your wishes are current.

In addition to what we might call the legal and official aspects of estate planning, there are some other things you might want to include. Instructions about your funeral are helpful to surviving family members, enabling them to make your memorial service the kind of witness you want it to be. You should also be sure to have a durable health-care power of attorney (including living-will choices); this will greatly reduce the pressure on your spouse and family of having to make unforeseen end-of-life decisions. Also, a financial power of attorney will streamline the oversight of details related to transferring your assets. Finally, you can write out other instructive information that is not legally binding per se, but is very helpful to others in knowing your wishes.

Perhaps the most important thing in estate planning is to talk with your spouse and children along the way. Creating as much of a common mind as possible in advance is a good strategy. And letting family members know basic information you have regarding legal and financial documents (including where they are located and related contact numbers to use in speaking with the managers of them) is a gift of efficiency to leave your heirs.

Chris, all of this should be done without any perception that you are trying to control things from the grave. Let your legal and financial counselors guide you in developing your estate plan with wording that communicates a good spirit as well as sound strategy. This is part of what we call "leaving a legacy." I learned a lot about this as my dad and father-in-law faced their own deaths. And I can tell you for sure that part of finishing well is dying well. Estate planning is one valuable expression of that.

Blessings!
Steve

Holy Dying

Dear Chris,

I wondered if my closing comment about death would spark any reply on your part. Honestly, I had not originally thought of including this in a series of letters about retirement. But as we have moved along, especially in our combination of spirituality and practicality, I have been thinking we would eventually come to the point of corresponding about it. Retirement is the phase of life when we look toward "the finish line" in the race God has set before us (Heb 12:1).

Our predecessors in the faith referred to this as "holy dying." It was a good thing for me years ago to explore some of the spiritual-formation literature (ancient and modern) about this. You may want to do the same. When I combine this literature with respect to retirement, the phrase used by my late mentor and friend Bishop Rueben Job comes to mind: living fully, dying well.[1] If what we have said about life before retirement and life after it is correct, then we should be on a trajectory that will make our entrance into heaven the culmination of a life well lived. Sometimes I think of it in this simple way: life, Life, LIFE.

But as with anything else, this is not an automatic progression. It comes with respect to certain key attitudes and actions. I think the most important is to embrace the reality of mortality. This is not

---

1. Rueben Job, *Living Fully, Dying Well* (Nashville: Abingdon Press, 2006).

having a death wish, but rather having a desire not to avoid the fact that we will die one day. There are so many ways that we deny death in our culture. But Christians should not be among those who do so, because we see death more as a doorway than a destination. One of the opportunities we have in retirement is to ponder our finitude, not in a morbid way, but in a way that sets our life in the context of eternity.

Another important thing is to make preparation for death. I live in Florida, and one of the things people do each year is to stockpile resources to get them through a hurricane. Food, water, batteries, propane, gasoline, and other necessities are at the ready. Thankfully, we don't have to use them all that often, but we know it is wise to have them on hand. Not long ago, I thought to myself that if I think it is important to prepare for a hurricane, wouldn't I also think it is important to prepare for my death? So, I "lay up treasures in heaven" by considering my going there one day.

One of the ways some of my friends have done this is by writing memoirs or their autobiographies. A few years ago, I did a version of this in a book entitled *When TV Came to Town*, a volume of about fifty stories describing my growing-up years in Haskell, Texas. I have a second volume in the works and some thoughts about a more re-flective memoir.

Not only is this a good gift to include in a legacy, but it is also a means to gather up the memories that have yielded values, virtues, and visions that are timeless in a very real sense of the word. Looking back upon our lives gives us the opportunity to recognize and rejoice in the fact that God has been making a new creation of us (2 Cor 5:17), one that will not end when our time on earth ends.

Chris, retirement is a time for developing perspective. And per-spective includes putting the days of our lives into an eternal context.

I think it is what the psalmist meant when he wrote, "Teach us to number our days so we can have a wise heart" (Ps 90:12). Far from being random, the days of our lives combine to create a journey— one that leads us to God's house (Ps 23:6).

Blessings!
Steve

Just the Two of Us

Dear Chris,

I am glad to hear that you and your spouse have been reading these letters together and that they have generated good conversation between you. As I have written previously, retirement is not something you are doing by yourself. Your spouse (and other family members as well) are on the journey too. I am glad to know you two are moving forward together in your discernment. I am happy to write in response to your invitation to say a bit more about marriage and retirement.

There is only one way that I can begin, and that is to share with you the fact that Jeannie has been my best friend, counselor, and encourager for more than forty-five years. Other than the Holy Spirit, her love and support has been the mainstay for my life and ministry. And many times, her love and counsel have been instruments the Holy Spirit has used to keep me heading in the right direction. I could write a book about all the ways she has devoted herself to making our life together what it has been. I will die with the blessing of having known what it was to be truly loved and to have had a wonderful marriage. With respect to retirement, this means that all our years together, in one way or another, have prepared us for this stage of life.

The fact that we have had a "talk, talk, talk" relationship means it was only natural that we would talk about retirement. And as I have already told you, we began to do that in earnest about seven years before I actually retired. Truth be told, we had talked about it even earlier as we both recognized the fact that "there has to be a last day." Preparing ourselves for that day before it actually came set all the intermediate work in a good context. But it was also necessary to focus our conversation on retirement when the prospect of it was nearer and the details were more relevant.

The most important thing for me to recognize was that my retirement would affect Jeannie as much as it would affect me. Her role as my wife has included huge amounts of ministry in her own right, the exercise of the particular gifts of the Spirit that she has, and the related adjustments that have occurred for her. As is the case with me, some of her ministries could continue in retirement, but many of the role-related ones had to be ended, just as mine did. So, we have had conversations about things related to the endings of what might be called our professional life together. And because Jeannie has never allowed herself to be role defined, we came to "the last day" with a good sense of our personhood separate from the tasks we had done for so long.

In terms of our personal life together, one of the hardest things for Jeannie was having a reasonable assurance that my "being at home all the time" would not require her to lose her own sense of space and significance. The fact is, I was invading *her* space, not the other way around. We had to talk about possible ways that both of us would have separate lives, as we have had over the years, without those becoming separations that negatively affect our relationship.

We have worked it out in the early years by respecting each other's space, particularly every morning—sometimes working in separate rooms so we are not looking over each other's shoulders all the time. That distance enables us to move along parallel lines with respect to our distinctive interests and the like. But we are also close enough to talk back and forth as each of us makes discoveries that we want to share. The larger sense that ours is a "life together" remains, but through different expressions.

Another important thing for us was for Jeannie to know that she could "go or not go" to things I agree to do. Even though I have never felt she attended things with me out of a sense of obligation— in fact, quite the opposite—we nevertheless realized that it was both an illusion and a mistake for me to think, *Now that I am retired, we can go everywhere together.* That is simply not true, and it never has been. As always, she has continued to be my best prayer partner, whether present or absent. I never go somewhere without her saying, "Preach the word!" And I often find little encouragement notes in my Bible or briefcase when I travel. That support, backed up with phone calls when I am on the road, has both given me the ongoing encouragement I need from her and provided her with the freedom to let me "hit the road" without her. Being joined in the heart does not require being joined at the hip!

I think what this actually means is that we needed to give each other a "no obligation" relationship, so that whatever we do together (or not do) flows from the same genuineness that has accompanied our marriage for so long. The fact is, we are just as much two individuals as we have ever been, and one of the grace gifts in retirement is to honor that in each other the best we can. Jeannie certainly has continued to do that for me, and I pray I am doing it for her.

Another important thing for us has been to have separate friendships. Of course, some of them overlap. But in our early years of retirement, I have continued to have some male friends and she has continued to have some female friends. We have not tried to blend everything together, and that has been a good thing. I go hiking with a friend each month, for example. And she meets with one of her friends to have lunch or to walk on one of the nearby trails. We have other friends we get with independently, and those moments are valuable and important to preserve.

Chris, I am sure there are other things I could add. But as I bring this letter to a close, I am mindful that the main thing in the marriage dimension of retirement is being able to define our life by the word *human* more than by the word *ministry*. Jeannie and I both know that ministry will not disappear from either of our lives, because we have committed ourselves to be disciples until the day we die. But with so many professional responsibilities laid aside, it opens up life in ways that are exciting and meaningful. We are still in the "go-go" phase of older adulthood, even though we know this will evolve into what others call the "slow-go" and "no-go" phases. We are experiencing the happiness of being able to do this together.

Chris, you and your spouse have the opportunity to follow the map of life into retirement as two people who love each other as much now as ever. As I have tried to say to you repeatedly in these letters, abundant life continues in retirement—and that is true for the two of you together.

Blessings!
Steve

You Have Much to Look Forward To

Dear Chris,

You ask about my association with other retired clergy, or those anticipating it as you are. I do have some relationships like that, and I am happy to write you about what they have shared with me. I have woven some of their experiences into previous letters, but recently I received some additional input focusing specifically on the positive things they have experienced in their early days of their retirement. In a nutshell, they say there is a lot to look forward to in retirement. I hope their witness will add to what I have been sharing with you.

The thing they said the most is how retirement affords the opportunity to get out from under stressful situations. Years ago, I benefitted from the writings of Dr. Archibald Hart, who wrote a lot about ministry as a stress-related and loss-prone vocation.[1] Now, many years later, I do not see the stress levels diminishing for clergy; in fact, as the church becomes more marginalized in society and subject to rejection by the "nones" and abdication by the "dones," I see even higher stress levels in certain cases. Institutional maintenance,

---

1. One of the most helpful to me was his book *Adrenalin and Stress* (Dallas: Word Publishing Group, 1991).

including survival strategies, is extremely stressful. It is not an easy time to be a clergyperson.

Fellow clergy tell me that one of the great joys of retirement is to be able to lay down whatever stress they have lived under and feel the freedom that comes from doing so. Most of us have learned to accommodate ourselves to the routine stressors, and we have gained coping skills for the unexpected crises that come in ministry. But that does not mean we have escaped the "erosion" of heart, soul, mind, and strength that living under stress for a long time creates. What I find interesting in the remarks of the other clergy, and in my own experience, is how quickly a sense of freedom (that perhaps we didn't even realize we needed) arises and begins to give a "lightness" to our being and a vigor to the day.

A second thing fellow clergy have told me is that they have experienced the joys that come with being part of a local congregation in a new way. I have not heard from clergy friends who either went on a staff part-time in retirement or took a small church. So, I don't have anything in this letter to share with you about that. Those I have heard from have moved from the pulpit to the pew, and the move has been good for them. Most of those who have gotten in touch have taken a "time-out" for upwards of a year, rather than jumping into a job like teaching Sunday school or visiting shut-ins. For most, it has been decades since they have been part of a congregation without having to wear the mantle of professional ministry, and they like the feeling of being one among the rest.

The third thing I am hearing from other clergy is the joy of discovering activities they and their spouses can do together. I called attention to this in the last letter, but it is worth mentioning again. Some of these are increased expressions they were already doing, but in some instances, they have found new things to do together. Added to this is the fact that some clergy retire before their spouses do, and they tell me that it is a joy to be in a supportive role to their spouses similar to the kind of support they have received from their spouse for so long.

Chris, it all flows together into a single word—*freedom.* The sense of freedom that comes with retirement unlocks many doors and creates a sense that there are new opportunities to be discovered, explored, and enacted. I was having coffee with a friend recently, and as I was describing how things were going, he responded by saying, "Steve, what all this says to me is that you are living as a free man." As I sat there, I realized he had spoken out loud what I was feeling on the inside. I am free—free to live life without all the preconceived schedules and expectations, free to recognize that the kingdom of God is broad as well as deep. This freedom generates the sense that life is expansive and wide—that God is present and active in people and things in ways that my focus upon the church (or in my case, the academy) did not always make so clear.

You have a lot to look forward to in retirement. That is what other clergy have been telling me, and it is what I want to pass on to you as we continue to delve into the details that go along with retiring.

Blessings!
Steve

God with Us in the Details

Dear Chris,

Yes, I remember the old adage that the best way to eat an elephant is a bite at a time. I like your sense that approaching retirement is a bite-after-bite experience. This keeps retirement from seeming so large as to become overwhelming. Most of what we are talking about will be worked out in the "small stuff" category. Theologically, this means that God is in the details—one expression of "Emmanuel," which means "God with us."

One of the details is facing the fact that retiring is hard work. David McKenna captures this reality in his book *Retirement Is Not for Sissies*.[1] For one thing, he rightly notes that the concept of retirement is still relatively new in our society. A hundred years ago, almost no one retired in ways akin to the process that brings about ten thousand people a day into it in the United States alone. Except for those who were wealthy enough not to work, everyone else pretty much continued to work until the day they died. And even today, given economic realities for more than we might imagine, the idea of retirement is still only a dream people hope they might be able to do. We don't realize how fortunate we have been to be engaged in a vocation where salaries and benefits are sufficient to make retirement possible for us.

---

1. David McKenna, *Retirement Is Not for Sissies* (Newberg, OR: Barclay Press, 2008).

But the possibility of retirement does not mean that the wheels for it are greased and that moving down the track is an effortless process. I do not need to tell you that; you already know it, and you are at work to arrange the details into a workable timeline that moves you through your active years of ministry into your retired years. This letter is mainly to encourage you to "hang in there" and deal with the details as they arise.

McKenna calls it developing a game plan. I like that image because a good game plan does not line up each play in the game in some kind of predestined order. Rather, a good game plan simply describes good moves to make when certain things happen or when particular issues need to be dealt with. The coach carries the game plan up and down the field, calling plays in no predetermined order, but as field position, opportunities, and challenges call for certain actions.

I hope that what you and I have written about so far is helping you develop your game plan—your playbook—for retirement. As you do this, I think you will find that you will have good responses to the details as they arise, regardless of their order or degree. And as with any game plan, it is not a solo endeavor. You have a cadre of friends and advisors who can pass on to you the wisdom of good information and lived experience. Assemble your team and move ahead. And the hard work of retirement will be set in the context of any other sport—an effort that requires two halves, four quarters, or nine innings.

If any of us were the first person on earth to retire, the challenges would be formidable. But in my study and in my conversations with others, I have not raised a single issue that has not been addressed previously by someone. Despite the effort required, it is good to know that when we put our hand on the knob of the retirement door, it turns!

Blessings!
Steve

The Inner Voice

Dear Chris,

I am intrigued that you raise the detail of passion as one of the early ones you have recognized in your discernment regarding retirement. While I have no perfect knowledge about this, I can tell you that the resources I have read, the people I have spoken with, and my own personal experience all combine to say that there does come the moment when an inner sense that "it's time" emerges in the mind and heart. The fact that you have recognized this in yourself is significant. I believe God is with us in providing this kind of experience.

Here's one way I became aware of it. I found myself sitting in meetings that were largely about future trajectories for the seminary—things projected to unfold in a five-year or ten-year plan. While sitting there, the inner voice said, "You're not going to be here for that." Looking around the table, I realized that the future of the seminary was really in the hands of younger faculty and staff—not me. This did not mean I left the meeting or bailed out of the immediate actions that were connected with moving the school toward those goals. It only meant that I began increasingly to own the reality that I would not be employed long enough to see many of the things being talked about come to pass.

Chris, I think this is one way God has of getting our attention and putting things into perspective—and it is a good thing. We need to consider retirement in terms of a future that will exist after we are gone. In fact, if we have led well, we will not be content to cast visions that are either small enough for us to fulfill or large enough to require us hanging on longer. Institutional work is never finished. If you have been part of conversations and planning that seems to go beyond your personal tenure, that's a good thing. It is also a sign that your heart is recognizing the sacred difference between envisioning and accomplishing.

Unfortunately, I know pastors and professors who cannot see the future without seeing themselves in it. They convince themselves that every scenario requires their presence. So, they hang on beyond their prime. We have already corresponded about that. But we are at a point in this correspondence when it is important to emphasize it again. Your nudges to separate your present moment from the larger future is a good thing. Your inner voice is trying to get your attention.

I cannot speak for you, but I experienced this in a second way as well. Even though I never lost my sense of calling and the fulfillment that accompanies it, I did recognize a diminishment of passion for some of the tasks related to my teaching ministry. I never lost a passion for students or for engaging with them inside and outside of class; that lasted until my last day on the job. But I did recognize a decline in my desire to be on "the cutting edge" of my discipline and a diminishment of interest in serving on things such as faculty committees. The core of my vocation was holding, but some of the secondary matters were beginning to flake off. For me at least, that was one of the ways I recognized that I was getting close to the time of retiring.

David McKenna puts it this way: "Do I still have fire in my belly for the future of this organization?"[1] As soon as he posits the question, he adds that we must not let our hearts deceive us into a premature and unreal yes. Almost no one maintains the same high pitch to the very end of ministry. Instead, we recognize some decline, and we need to pay attention to this when we do. McKenna challenges those considering retirement to pay attention to the inner voice, because it is trying to speak both knowledge and wisdom into us. And as I said at the beginning of this letter, everyone I have talked with found themselves in a moment like I have described. Somehow they "knew" they needed to think about retiring.

Chris, I am glad you have acknowledged to yourself and to me that you are hearing that voice and attending to the stirrings it creates. This is a necessary step in your discernment and decision making. Otherwise, you may find yourself being guided by denial more than by the details that are trying to get your attention through the inner voice. If you give heed to that voice in a responsive (not reactive) way, you will always be glad you had "ears to hear" the messages coming your way.

Blessings!
Steve

---

1. David McKenna, *The Leader's Legacy* (Newberg, OR: Barclay Press, 2006), 68.

Putting It on a Timeline

Dear Chris,

I understand and agree with the need to eventually put all this on paper and create an actual timeline for your retirement. This is surely one of the unavoidable details in discerning the reality of your retirement and the schedule you should follow in executing it. I like your comment about the inner voice; that it is beginning to say, "Get a piece of paper and start writing this stuff down!" I know you have already been doing that, but there does come a time to turn notes into some kind of plan. I am happy to offer a few suggestions about this.

Because you and I are in the same denomination, there may be some direct correlation between the timeline I followed and the one that will work for you. But knowing that you are using these letters to have conversations with other clergy who are in other ecclesial arrangements, there may need to be some adjustments for them. I have written previously about this process in terms of the principles related to it; now, I will describe the way that things played out on the calendar, and particularly with respect to my ending my relationship as an active elder in The United Methodist Church.

In the late summer of 2012, I wrote a letter to my bishop (copied to my district superintendent), informing him of my desire to retire at the next Annual Conference, which was about ten months away. After the usual tongue-in-cheek "we are not going to let you do this," both of these men approved my request and told me some of the things I needed to do in order to make that agreement institutionally active.

Along with this, I contacted the General Board of Pensions, getting the information from them that I needed to keep the ball rolling. Within a few weeks, I had the approvals I needed and had in hand the basic outline I needed to follow. In October of that year, the General Board sent me a form letter, repeating some of the things I had already been told, but it was a confirmation that I was not lost in the system. I was on their radar screen for a retirement the following June.

Between October and June, several helpful things happened. Jeannie and I attended the pre-retirement seminar offered by the Annual Conference. And in January, the Conference Board of Ordained Ministry officially voted to approve my retirement. Also about that time, I received a retirement packet from the General Board of Pensions that had all the directions and forms I needed to finalize the process. By March, the General Board had connected me with one of their retirement specialists (who had received most of what I had filled out in the packet), and we had several helpful conversations that moved the process further toward completion. In one of those conversations, I discovered that the General Board had even more resources to offer, depending upon the specifics of my situation.

Between March and May, I completed all the forms and other required paperwork, sending everything to the retirement specialist for approval and to use the information to get me on schedule to begin receiving monthly pension payments, which began the first month (i.e., July) after the Annual Conference session that gave the final vote to my request to retire and included Jeannie and me (along with about thirty other retiring clergy) in its service to honor that year's retirees.

With all that being done, Jeannie and I came to the day at Annual Conference when we attended our first retiree luncheon and then moved on to be part of the actual service where more than thirty clergy and their spouses were recognized for their years of service and formally retired in the context of worship. So far, we have continued to attend that annual luncheon and retirement service, both because we know the folks who are retiring each year, but also as a way to say by our attendance, "Well done, good and faithful servants."

Chris, this process of turning principles into a timeline helped me arrange the maze of details into a workable program. The old adage "A place for everything and everything in its place" came true in my final year of service both as a clergyperson and as a teacher. You are already doing a good job compiling the major aspects of your retirement and committing yourself to them. I believe your confidence will only increase as you place these things on the calendar.

Growing up in West Texas, I learned enough about horses to know that when cowboys got lost, they would release the reins and "give the horse its head"—which meant letting the horse's instincts kick in and find the way home. For some reason, that analogy has come to my mind as I write this to you. So much of what we have shared back and forth has been about things you need to do, and they are important things. But you will come to the time when you release the reins and "give the system its head." Our denomination has gotten all sorts of clergy home, and it will do the same for you.

Blessings!
Steve

What If I'm Not Ready to Retire?

Dear Chris,

Wow! When I read the start of your letter, I had a shot of adrenaline go through me. I first wondered if I was going to have to do some triage on your spirit because something had gone wrong in the midst of all we have been sharing. I was happy to know that this is not the case for you but intrigued to learn that a couple of your friends are feeling they are not ready to retire. I am sure you have already been of great help to them, but I will accept your invitation to write some about what we can do when the feeling "I am not ready to retire" sweeps over us.

Your first friend describes his reluctance as more inward than outward. I am not surprised, because it is not easy to come to grips with the fact that something we have been doing for so long will soon come to an end—at least in the active, professional sense. In one of the early letters, I shared with you the painful experience some of us had with a colleague who "died a thousand deaths" in his final year of service. We hardly ever saw him in that last year without hearing some version of "this is the last time I will ever _____." It soon became a heavy sadness to bear, because we could so easily see that he was retiring kicking and screaming.

As you describe it, your friend is at this stage—the stage of inner reluctance. If that is the case, perhaps going back to the spiritual formation letters will help you remember some things that can be helpful to share. Assuming that your friend's earlier inclination to retire is legitimate, I hope that some reminders can get him over the hump and enable him to finish well. It is not unusual to have second thoughts; the discernment is whether these are temporary or indicative of a surfacing problem with respect to retirement.

If your friend's problem is a deeper denial, your task will be more difficult. I had to deal with this once with a colleague whom I supervised, and moving the person on to retirement required a more protracted and delicate process. You will have to decide how strong your friendship is, but you may have to "speak the truth in love" in order to break the log jam that has stopped your friend from fulfilling his decision. In the situation I had to face, the honesty included having to have conversations about the person's health and how the decline was not only making a continuation of ministry difficult for him but also making it increasingly challenging for those around him who worked with him and for him. Happily, these conversations took place while the person was able to see what we were pointing out; and because he loved us more than he loved his job, he did not become overly defensive when we had to nudge him to move on into retirement.

It could be that your friend's denial is not related to anything physical, but you will have to review with him whatever conditions you (and likely, others as well) believe are relevant for him not to ignore. In some cases, you may be able to start with things your friend has previously articulated. When retirement is not staring us in the face, we can be remarkably realistic about ourselves and our situation. Perhaps saying, "Do you remember when you told me that…?" might be a way to return to a reality your friend has lost as anxiety and downright fear have begun to define the situation.

Sometimes the recovery of an earlier dream or insight can be enough to get things back on track. I hope so.

Turning to your second friend, the issue appears to be a kind of reality check when he ran the economic numbers. It is a reminder that there are many clergy who, though eligible for retirement, simply do not have the resources to do so. In general, I would simply say that this is the time for you to encourage your friend to engage more aggressively with a financial advisor, to have conversations with any of his friends who were worried (like him) about money matters, and to also have conversations with denomination pension counselors who might be able to suggest alternatives. If your friend is willing to do this, I imagine he can reframe the picture. But you can also be ready to offer some general advice that might help and will likely correspond with what he learns from others.

For example, your friend can actually postpone his retirement (assuming his economic challenges are real and formidable) and allow pension and social security benefits to increase in value. This does not mean postponing the Medicare enrollment we wrote about earlier; he must do that at age sixty-five. But a financial advisor or denominational retirement counselor can help your friend run the numbers on current investments and what a year-by-year postponement would mean.

The only caution I offer here is that any of us can easily say, "Well, my advisor told me that if I wait to retire, I will have more money to live on." That's always true (assuming investments do not tank), but it can also be a psychological placebo a person can use to justify postponing retiring. Unless there are legitimate economic concerns, it means your friend has gotten a case of "cold feet" and needs the advice and wisdom of an outside party to help him see things differently.

The economics of retirement can also be helped by factoring in some new income streams that your friend may not have thought he needed to consider when he first began to think about retiring. His denomination may have some options, but there can also be some income-producing options in the marketplace as well. Here may be an occasion for your friend to talk with members of his church to see what might be available. Here is one of those "you have not because you ask not" moments. There may be laity in your friend's congregation who can offer post-retirement employment (if your friend has chosen to remain in the community) or provide suggestions for continuing to earn some money in retirement.

Another often-used strategy is to increase savings in the years leading up to retirement. We talked about some possibilities in a previous letter. But I now remember a former student telling me that when he finally finished paying off his student loans, he and his wife decided not to simply "beef up" their monthly budget but to invest a portion of the money they had already become accustomed to paying the government back each month, so that that their retirement funds would grow faster and larger.

Another alteration can be with respect to housing. Your friend and his wife may be able to reconsider what kind of home or apartment to live in once they retire. A smaller house will not cost as much, and the annual costs (e.g., taxes and utilities) will also be less. This does not mean settling for something inferior. Regardless of how your friend handles this, he needs to discuss home-equity loan options that may release funds that he had not considered previously. A banker or financial planner will be able to help your friend decide what the best risk/benefit formula is for him with regard to things like this.

Chris, if you find other contributing factors in your friends' hesitation, we can talk about them. I will join you in prayer, asking God to give you wisdom to stand on the foundation of the friendship you have with each of these people and walk along with them through the giving of love and the best counsel you can offer. The thing for you to remember—and to help them remember as well—is that there has to be a "last day." Whether their hesitation is internal or external (or a mix of the two), the reassessment must be in relation to that reality, not the avoidance of it. I am sure there are some clergy who have no option but to work until they die. But from what you have told me, that does not seem to be the case with either of your friends. Instead, their challenge is to name their gremlin and get good advice relative to it. Your presence with them as they do this will be a great grace gift.

Blessings!
Steve

Shepherding the Flock

Dear Chris,

The care you are giving to your own retirement includes shepherding your flock through the transition process. You and I have been part of an appointive process where we periodically participate in "moving day"—the day when a gaggle of clergy families leave one place and go to their next church. And while this is institutionally efficient, and while we have accustomed ourselves to being part of the process from time to time, I do not think we have sufficiently explored the dynamics created among the clergy and the related congregation when this is taking place.

Loading early in the morning in the familiar place and unloading later in the day in the unfamiliar place is not enough time for either pastor or people to process everything that is happening. Even good moves include leaving behind and carrying forward "invisible baggage" that has the potential to leave both clergy and congregation with issues that must be addressed. I am not sure this can be eliminated completely, but I do think there are some things we can do to make the transition process better for ourselves and for those we are leaving.

Let me start with the obvious. Has your congregation ever experienced a clergy retirement? Most churches simply say good-bye to a pastor and family who are going on to a new assignment. But that is not going to be the case with you and your congregation. If they have had previous clergy retire in their midst, find out what they did to celebrate that reality and symbolize the occasion for themselves and their pastoral family. Find out what went well. Don't be surprised if you find out that little was done; here is your opportunity to leave a legacy by creating an experience they can draw on should they ever have another pastor retire.

But if they have had someone retire, you may be able to draw from things that were said and done in order to make your retirement personally and congregationally meaningful. There may also be some community dimensions to this as well, especially in those places the clergyperson has served beyond the walls of the congregation. The farewell process should give the opportunity to be involved to everyone who needs it.

A second legacy gift you can give your people is to function as something of an "interim" pastor. Obviously, you are not that in the technical sense, so let me explain what I mean. An increasing number of larger churches are making use of interims to bridge the transition between pastors. There are a lot of good things that can come of this approach.[1] Your church will not likely use an interim in the formal sense, although it may be something you will at least want to learn more about. You can use what you find out in your final months in the congregation to help make the transition better. I believe there are three things that are especially important.[2]

First, find ways throughout the congregation to identify the strengths of the past. You have been in your church long enough to

---

1. You can go online and get specific information on the role of interim pastors. A good starting point is www.interimpastors.com. The Presbyterian Church (USA) also has good information and resources for an interim pastor experience (http://oga.pcusa.org).

2. I am indebted to the insights given me by David McKenna in this phase of transition, many of which he has written about in his book *The Leader's Legacy* (Newberg, OR: Barclay Press, 2006).

know what some of these are. But use your final months to ask others to share their memories with you. Use your final rounds of pastoral visitation to ask people to tell you what they perceive key strengths to be. You can encourage classes and groups to devote time to identifying the strengths resident in their part of the congregation. Have folks compile lists and give them to you. As things come to light, you can develop worship services to highlight the strengths that exist and will enable the congregation to stand on a good foundation as the next chapter of their life together begins to be written.

In terms of your personal ministry, the important thing that begins to happen in this phase is that the focus is taken off of you and what you have done and is placed on the church. This is very important, and it is a mark of pastoral integrity not to leave a congregation so entwined with you that the next pastor inevitably falls prey to "death by comparison." Identifying congregational strengths puts the church in the hands of the people, which is where it needs to be as they say good-bye to you and hello to someone else.

A second dimension of your interim work is to help the congregation sense momentum in the present. Do not overplan activities, but don't create a vacuum either. Be sure that key ministries will be "alive and well" when the new pastor arrives. Don't make your successor guess what needs to be done next. Work with your staff-parish committee to create tangible welcome signs for the new family, and schedule the public welcoming event or events that can help your successor become familiar with and assimilated into the new appointment.[3] One good thing you can do is to have a meal

---

3. Tangible welcome signs could include such things as finding out what each family member likes and have an item related to that waiting for them. For example, if a child likes a certain toy, have it or something related to it on one of the beds. You can do this for each person who is moving in. Also, find out if anyone is having a birthday shortly after they move in, and don't let it pass without giving cards and gifts to celebrate the day that would likely otherwise go unnoticed. If the pastor and spouse will soon have an anniversary, be ready to give them a

plan in place for the first week or so, because the energy of the family will be spent on unpacking. The point is, things like this are signs of momentum to the congregation and signs of attentiveness to the new pastor.

Beyond the early welcoming events, you should also help your congregation have a healthy sense of its mission—not one that ties the hands of your successor, but rather one that does not keep him or her in the dark about the leading edges of vision and strength in the congregation. You have spent years on this. Do not turn it into guesswork for whoever follows you. Work with key lay leaders, helping them compile and be ready to articulate missional dynamics related to the parts of the congregation they are involved with. Be sure to make it clear to your laity that this information will not be given to the incoming pastor as a set of "expectations" (and surely not as potential items to use in evaluating him or her), but rather as "windows" through which to look in order to set foot into the congregation and see it as an engaged body of believers.

A third dimension of your interim work is to help your congregation trust that their future is in the hands of God and that the potential for doing new and even greater things is there. One of the ways that I tried to do this was to preach a closing series of sermons on each of the membership vows, reminding the congregation what they had pledged to do, showing them how those promises had served the church well during my tenure, and inviting all who would to recommit to giving their devotion of prayers, presence, gifts, and service to the next pastor. We had a weekly prayer time at the altar after each sermon, so people could recommit themselves to a particular

---

gift or some time away—again, something new churches would not know about unless they ask. The chair of the staff-parish committee can gather this basic information and then bring it to the church for creative implementation.

vow. On the final Sunday, the whole service was planned to enact the congregation's reaffirmation of their vows.[4]

Chris, while you will never refer to yourself as an interim (because you are not), you can use your closing year in the congregation to build a bridge that is anchored in the good work you and your people have done together and that is now extended into the future as the new pastor continues to oversee the journey. It is like a team race at a track event. The likelihood of a win is increased as team members learn about and practice good handoffs. You play a key role in this as you shepherd the flock into a sense that the mission of the church is in view, momentum to continue it is in place, and morale is high enough to move the congregation forward. The greatest gift you can give your people is trust in God, which translates to mean that they can move ahead without you, while at the same time honoring and advancing the good work that has occurred while you were together.

Blessings!
Steve

---

4. In the Wesleyan tradition, some churches use the Covenant Renewal Service as a way to do this—or an adaptation of it.

Get Out of the Way

Dear Chris,

I hesitate to write you about this, because I do not want you to think I have any concerns about your willingness or ability to "get out of the way." Also, I have made mention of this need in a previous letter. I am writing again about it because I have heard from clergy who have identified a former pastor's inability to "get out of the way" as a formidable hindrance to their ministry. Sometimes, it is something the former pastor is not sufficiently aware of; at other times it is a further expression of an inability to let go. Either way, it is a serious challenge we must not leave to chance.

In an earlier letter, I told you that one of the great lessons given me by David McKenna is the principle to "go away and stay away." Even before he chiseled it in stone for me, I found that I had been largely practicing the principle by instinct. But once we had the opportunity to visit about it, and I saw David's determination to enact the principle, I became even more convinced it is the better way. With David's wisdom and witness in place in my life, I began to notice clergy who (in my opinion) hung around too much after they retired, either by continuing to attend the church they had just pastored or by coming back for some things the new pastor should have been involved with. I know there are legitimate reasons for some of this. That is not my concern in this letter. What I want to address is the problem of unnecessarily or excessively "casting a shadow" that hangs over your successor.

In my case, as a retiring seminary professor, I did not have the congregational dynamic to deal with as local pastors do. But I have had to be intentional about not casting a shadow over the campus where I taught and served as an administrator for fifteen years or over the seminary where I taught since 1980. Of course, there are people and things that we miss. But trying to stay involved and aware only creates a higher risk of trying to exert influence I no longer have, and I have absolutely no desire to do that.

Moreover, going away and staying away keeps me from knowing how things are changing. It is inevitable that they will change when a new pastor or leader moves into their time of service. But some of the changes are not necessarily ones you would approve of, and even if you do, the changes may be implemented in ways you would not have chosen. It is much simpler and less unsettling not to be monitoring these changes. So, here is another reason why going away and staying away is a good thing.

Chris, I want to repeat what I said at the beginning of the letter: there are legitimate things to return to your church to do. I would think, for example, that if you have done the premarital counseling with a couple whom you have come to know well, it would be appropriate for you to return to officiate at their wedding. But I would be sure to have the couple consider a way the new pastor can be present and involved, for he or she will be the one who will be caring for them after the wedding. I can also imagine that there might be a few funerals that would involve you. But as a general rule, I would say yes to a future request only through the invitation of the current pastor. A simple "Have you spoken with your pastor about this?" is good enough to complete the loop, making your involvement part of the new reality.

If you have ever had a previous pastor hang around when you moved into your time of ministry, you will understand what I am talking about. You will know how delicate but important it is to make a gracious exit. Your own well-being will be enhanced by doing so, and the spirit of your successor will be much healthier if he or she does not feel you are watching every move and evaluating it. When I retired, another professor who retired before I did and moved away would occasionally call to see how Jeannie and I were doing and to ask, "How are things going at the seminary?" I noticed that after a while, he stopped calling, and the two of us later joked that he eventually realized I was not a source of ongoing information! I simply did not know what was going on.

I believe this is a good thing. It does mean some may not understand your decision to be so separated from what you were once so close to. But that is a better price to pay than having your successor hamstrung and your people confused by your ongoing presence in the congregation, or maybe (as I know a few to have done), remaining in the building as you set up shop in a retirement office of some kind.

Chris, the simplest thing I can say is this: don't do it!

Blessings!
Steve

The Life-Giving Combination

Dear Chris,

If there is a single thread I have tried to keep running through all our letters, it is this: there is life after retirement. But that does not mean you can avoid sadness as you retire; in fact, you will likely experience it in waves. This is completely normal, unless it becomes debilitative for you in some way. And in that normality, I would urge you to receive your sadness as an indication that you have given yourself genuinely to those whom you have served in the current congregation, as well as a sign of your investment in those you have served over the years.

I would be surprised and disappointed if you could walk away with no sadness. I have to tell you, I wished in every place that there did not have to be a final service or farewell occasion. But then I jokingly realized that if we eliminated the final Sunday, the next-to-the-last one would suddenly become the last one! There is simply no way I know of to avoid some tears. Both you and your people need to shed them. Any transition includes emotion, and retirement adds some additional factors to the mix. But returning to the principle of "life" running through our correspondence, I believe there is a life-giving combination that can serve you well.

I find it in the words of Paul—the passage in which he writes to Timothy and says two things: "I have...Henceforth" (2 Tim 4:7-8

KJV). When I came to the time of retirement, these two things enabled me to look to the past with realistic joy and to look toward the future with genuine anticipation. I believe this is a dynamic duo. It is a mixture that creates perspective, both for you and your people.

Chris, I encourage you to do some gathering. It might be journals you have kept over the years, photos that have marked your years of service, or letters and papers that honor your ministry in some way. One of the things I did was to go through my calendars and compile a list of the places where I had preached and taught. Jeannie surprised me with two special notebooks—one when I turned sixty, and one when I retired. These are filled with precious memories that I can turn to quickly, and one page after another not only bears witness to my life and work but opens the door to additional recollections.

One of the things Dr. Ellsworth Kalas did for decades is to go back to his hometown each year and walk the streets, remembering people and things who gave him the start that led to so many other things. After you retire, you might want to travel to each of the churches you have served, and without notice and fanfare, just spend some relaxed and unhurried time on the grounds and in the community. I will leave it to you to decide what kinds of things you want to gather to help you give thanks for the ways God has used you. Whatever you decide to do will be your version of "I have..." that Paul recounted for Timothy.

And then, begin to compile your "henceforth" list. You can do it drawing on some of the things we have explored in previous letters, and perhaps we can look together at other elements that can give us life in the early years of retirement. Your "henceforth" list will include those things you are looking forward to doing. Jeannie and I recently had lunch with a clergyperson and his spouse who have become members of a boat-rental club that will allow them to go to any number of places, secure a vessel, and go out on a lake or along the coast to enjoy fishing and sailing. As I have said in some earlier letters, the sky is the limit for things like this. The important thing is to begin to identify real things that can pull you into early retirement with a sense of anticipation. Paul's "crown of righteousness" (2 Tim 4:8 KJV) is not merely something that awaited him in heaven but also something he could wear with joy in this life. Your ministerial righteousness ought to have future enjoyments as well as past precious memories. This is your "henceforth" list.

Chris, I have found that the "I have...henceforth" combination has increased the sense of life, which as I have said repeatedly in these letters is the essence of the Christian faith in its personal and professional expressions. I look back with genuine happiness as I recall many of the things that have confirmed the validity of the calling that got me started in ordained ministry in the first place. And I look forward with true joy as I see doors opening and opportunities abounding.

Blessings!
Steve

Becoming More Meditative

Dear Chris,

I agree. The last letter was a kind of entering "the home stretch" of our correspondence. We have corresponded about many things, and as you like in the future, we can continue to do so. But using the "I have...henceforth" combination creates wholeness to what we have been considering—an invitation to use whatever upcoming communication we have to draw things together and bring our sharing to a good conclusion.

To use Paul's "I have...henceforth" combination is to become more meditative. My favorite definition of *meditation* came to me through Evelyn Underhill, who called it "mental prayer."[1] I like that because I do most of my processing through my thoughts. It was good to know that as I consecrate my thoughts to God, I am practicing a classical form of meditation. For me at least, this is close to what others refer to when they speak of mindfulness or paying attention. This kind of meditation creates the intersection of *chronos* and *kairos*, making sacred the here and now of my life.

Along the way, I have gathered other mentors to assist me in my meditation. I must mention the writings of Thomas Merton, Thomas Keating, and Richard Rohr. Merton's book on meditation

---

1. Evelyn Underhill and Charles Lewis Slattery, *Concerning the Inner Life* (New York: E. P. Dutton & Company, 1947), 37.

has been one that I return to for a kind of "refresher course" on the subject.[2] And as I have already told you, retirement has increased the opportunities for me to be more meditative.

I have more time to be pensive—more time to penetrate the surface of things. A hot cup of coffee can be a call to worship, a call to be still and know God—a time to ponder a particular idea rather than just look at it briefly. It also means that I can spend more time with impressions that come as I move through the day.

Chris, as we begin to wind down our correspondence, I don't think I could write about anything more important than that of using retirement for increased meditation. I think it is what the Bible means by gaining wisdom (Ps 90:12), and scripture shows that this is a particular opportunity for older people. We have time to turn knowledge into wisdom. We can become *elders* in fact, not just in title. I covet this experience for you when you move into retirement. I am confident that you will find it to be so.

Blessings!
Steve

---

2. Thomas Merton, *Spiritual Direction and Meditation* (Collegeville, MN: The Liturgical Press, 1960). It has been subsequently re-issued, including an e-book format.

Remaining Active

Dear Chris,

Becoming more meditative does not mean being less active, and it certainly does not mean beginning to live in the past. Nor does it mean "staying busy" as some attempt to convince ourselves that our lives still have value. Hopefully, I have said enough in our previous letters to show that I have something else in mind when I write about remaining active. As we wind down our correspondence, I think it is important to emphasize maintaining an active lifestyle. Of course, I mean remaining active physically and continuing to take care of ourselves. We have already pointed to such things. I have something else in mind now. Let me share a few of the ways I am remaining active in retirement.

First, I am rereading books that spoke powerfully to me in the past. At first glance, this may seem like living in the past, but it is not. Rather, I am rereading formative literature in order to discover what it has to say to me now. In some cases, I was a young man when these books influenced my life. Decades have passed. Reading some of these books again is to do so from an entirely different vantage point. It is exploring formative "gold mines" to see what else they have to yield. And from a practical standpoint, it means not having to spend as much on new books! (But I confess I am still buying more than I probably should.)

Another way I am remaining active is by increasing my connections with current reality through social media. I am somewhat hesitant to mention this, because I see so much misuse of social media. But with a planned involvement in it, the use of Google searches and the reading of valuable social sites affords a way to "stay in touch" with people and ideas that are shaping the present. Again, most of this is free. You don't have to spend a lot of money on subscriptions, dues, and so forth. Additionally, various periodicals also have e-letters you can receive and Facebook pages you can access. I find these things helpful not only as a way to remain connected with ideas that have been of longstanding interest, but also as a way of opening doors for exploring new things.

Third, I am keeping key friendships active. I mentioned that earlier, but now is a good time to highlight it. Retirement does not require that we end all our past relationships. I am maintaining a number of friendships that not only get me out of the house but also keep key relationships alive in the present. These include both clergy and laity. In addition to what I am doing, I know a group of clergy who plan regular times to be together. Some have retired and others are approaching it. They have been together for decades. Their latest gathering was a fishing trip off the coast of Florida.

Fourth, Jeannie and I are enjoying service to others. One way we do this is through financial support of people we know who are in active ministries that we feel led to support. This not only keeps our financial stewardship alive but also keeps us engaged with ministries that are making a difference in ways that we are not able to at this time of our life. Additionally, we serve along with members of our local church in a ministry to the homeless. And as I am writing this to you, Jeannie and I are discerning how to increase our service time through other volunteer opportunities. We do not want this to become another form of "busyness," so we are moving slowly and carefully. But at the same time we recognize that retirement affords opportunities for service that the past did not.

Chris, these things are enough to illustrate the principle of mixing meditation and activity in retirement. As I told you in a previous letter, we live out this combination through the way we spend our mornings and afternoons. It is a lifestyle that can be scheduled. But as we do this, we find remaining active to be an expression of the social holiness to which we have given ourselves throughout our past, even if in different ways. You will not have any difficulty finding your own formative activities in retirement. They are all around. As you do this, you will find joy and flat-out fun in doing so. And from a place deep within, I believe you will hear the Spirit say, "Well done, good and faithful servant."

Blessings!
Steve

Finding a Flexible Future

Dear Chris,

In a previous letter, I told you about the friend who looked at me and said that he saw a "free man" in my retirement. As I have pondered his statement, I think the primary way I am experiencing that freedom is in terms of flexibility. In retirement I am able to "arrange things" in ways I have never been able to do before. That is true freedom. And when the things we have said about spiritual formation are woven into the picture, it is not a selfish freedom, but one that creates a sacred flexibility.

Flexibility means that retirement is largely about staying open. The best-laid plans cannot presume to include every eventuality that life will bring your way. I trust I have already communicated this sense of anticipation in previous letters. But given your affirmation of what I am saying, I want to double down and encourage you to move into the future with hope.

One of the reasons I agreed to correspond with you about retirement is that I believe it is a phase of life to anticipate going deeper into everything good that God has placed in your life and a season to plant new seeds that only retirement can give you. That is one reason why you are wise in wanting to combine spirituality and practicality in your retirement plan. Both are necessary, and together they combine to give life a continuing sense of future and hope (Jer 29:11). I want that for you. In the Wesleyan tradition it is what we call practical divinity.

I have found that a flexible future means capitalizing on the opportunity to pursue a keen interest with increased fervor. From talking with people in retirement, I have learned that this increase can connect with anything: a vocational or avocational interest, a hobby, or the opening of a door to something you have previously expressed a desire to do "someday." A flexible future also means being open to surprises—to things unexpected, to brand-new things you might never have thought about doing before you retired.

I also think that a flexible future means not seeing the aging process and its inevitable slowing down as something to be feared, denied, or resisted. If this comes with sickness or disability, I know it means having to deal with challenges. But even then, God is with us. A flexible future includes adapting to the value found in fewer things. Perhaps one way to put it is that living into a flexible future includes savoring life, not consuming it—swimming in it, not skiing on it. I am not far enough into retirement to have a good sense of this, but I know from talking with others farther down the retirement path than I am, that a sense of openness and flexibility is important. Focus will occur, and limitations eventually come, both by choice and necessity. But embracing a "less is more" flexibility will not only serve you well in the present moment, it will be a solid rock to stand on when (as St. Francis described it) Brother Donkey will not take you as far and as fast as he used to.

Chris, the soul is more like a balloon than a jar. It can move with the wind, not just sit on a shelf. The winds of retirement will blow in directions and with speeds none of us can predict, and surely not control. But we can respond and move along. That is exactly the kind of flexibility I am discovering in retirement. I am confident that you will too.

Blessings!
Steve

Closing Metaphors

Dear Chris,

Before we bring our correspondence to a close, I want to be sure to share two metaphors that have become meaningful for me in retirement: tending a garden and hoisting a sail. Each one has enabled important truths about retirement to remain in my mind.

Thinking of retirement as tending a garden has reminded me that there are things to cultivate and things to eliminate. Joan Chittister's book *The Gift of Years* has provided me with many examples of this.[1] She does not use the gardening metaphor, but she does write meditatively about things to grow and things to weed out. Like a garden, she arranges her book with a mixture of such things, rather than having two separate categories. The way she writes reminds me how life is a mixture, and that we never come to the end of needing to sort through the things that are making us better and the things that are not. I think you would find her book helpful.

Thinking of retirement as tending a garden further reminds me that each time I work on life, I keep turning up new things. And I am reminded that my life, like a garden, has seasons and I must not expect everything to grow at once. I must also not panic when a "winter" season sets in, when nothing much seems to be happening.

1. Joan Chittister, *The Gift of Years* (New York: BlueBridge, 2008).

In fact, there are times when being "unproductive" is exactly what I need.

A second metaphor that has helped me in retirement is raising a sail. Emilie Griffin's book *Souls in Full Sail* has provided me with additional good insight for retirement.[2] She helped me see even more clearly that retirement is not a time to take down our sails and tether our ship to the dock, but rather a time to hoist the sails and allow the Holy Spirit to send us on journeys that include returning to some of the former places, but also venturing into new ones. I want to offer you the hoisted-sail metaphor.

Biblically, I believe both metaphors relate to key ideas. Tending a garden connects me with the idea of water and how necessary it is for a crop to grow. And so I pray, "God, rain in me so that I may bear good fruit in retirement." Raising a sail is a reminder that it is the Holy Spirit who blows into my life, moving me forward on the journey of life. And so I pray, "Come, Holy Spirit, and fill my soul so that it may move in response to you." Even before I retired, the metaphor of the raised sail was important for me.[3]

Both metaphors are essentially invitations to trust God. We do not understand how seeds grow, and (as Jesus said) we do not know how the wind blows. Life is a mystery, but life is not meaningless. Chris, you have lived and taught that "God is the ruler yet." Retirement is going to be a time for you to believe that more than ever and to receive "produce" from your soul's garden and "power" from your sail's unfurling.

Blessings!
Steve

---

2. Emilie Griffin, *Souls in Full Sail: A Christian Spirituality for the Later Years* (Downers Grove, IL: InterVarsity Press, 2011).

3. I have tried to describe this more fully in my book *Fresh Wind Blowing* (Eugene, OR: Wipf and Stock, 2013).

Heading toward the Dawn

Dear Chris,

It has been a joy and privilege to correspond with you about retirement. I send you this final letter as my promise to continue to pray for you as you live toward the time when you retire and as you live into the days immediately following. As I have thought about this final letter, I have continued to hold the metaphors of garden-tending and sail-hoisting in my mind. Both gardeners and sailors like to operate in quieter and cooler times of day. Both are inspired to keep heading for the dawn. I offer you this third metaphor as we bring these letters to an end.

Gardeners and sailors are pilgrims on a journey that has no end. Their actions may be simple or complex. They do what needs to be done when it needs to be done. Gardeners and sailors are both oriented to the light and they work and navigate well in it. Whatever retirement is, it is walking in the light as God is in the light (1 John 1:7) and trusting that by doing so we will find each step ordered by God. Retirement is looking for that light in every moment and making a beeline toward it.

This is not hopeless naiveté; it is faith. Of course, there will be days when the clouds hide the sun. But the sun is still there. Light is still shining. And on most days, even when it is cloudy, we can still recognize the general vicinity of the sun. Using the gardening metaphor, there will be days when it does not rain, but the soil still holds moisture to make things grow. Using the sailing metaphor here, there are days when the wind does not blow, but we can still tell one direction from another.

I like the metaphor of heading toward the dawn because it also enables me to recognize that life unfolds slowly. The sun does not "pop up"; it rises. If you are up before dawn, you can trace the rising by the change in colors from darkness to a full light spectrum—a rising that has the emergence of multiple colors, each adding beauty to the moment and merging into the larger sunrise. Even after sunrise, the sun journeys across the sky with marked moments of additional wonder and beauty, often ending with a sunset more spectacular than anything else seen during the day. At any time, there is plenty to see. Chris, there is as much light in retirement as there has ever been in your life. Every sunset in one place is a sunrise in another place. Yes, the sun is setting on the terrain of your life called professional ministry, but it is rising in the territory called older adulthood. So, head for the dawn!

Thank you for inviting me to explore life in retirement. It has been a spiritual exercise for me to think about my retirement and share thoughts with you. But even our best descriptions fall short. Some things are beyond words. Other things can only be processed by living them, not speaking about them. Retirement is the continuation of asking, seeking, and knocking that you have been doing for so long. Pray for me as I continue to do this in my future years of retirement, and be assured that I will be praying for you as well.

Chris, if these letters have done what I originally hoped they would, they will have given you the confidence to "step aside," but to do so with full assurance that you will then "move ahead." And so it is with all who walk with God, no matter what stage of life we are in!

Blessings!
Steve

For Further Reading

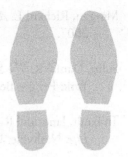

Bianchi, Eugene. *Aging as a Spiritual Journey.* New York: Crossroad, 1985.

Buchanan, Missy. *Talking with God in Old Age.* Nashville: Upper Room Books, 2010.

Chittister, Joan. *The Gift of Years.* New York: BlueBridge, 2008.

Griffin, Emilie. *Souls in Full Sail.* Downers Grove, IL: InterVarsity Press, 2011.

Harper, Steve. *Fresh Wind Blowing.* Eugene, OR: Wipf and Stock, 2013.

Hinden, Stan. *How to Retire Happy.* New York: McGraw Hill, 2013.

Job, Rueben. *Living Fully, Dying Well.* Nashville: Abingdon Press, 2006.

McKenna, David. *The Leader's Legacy.* Newberg, OR: Barclay Press, 2006.

———. *Retirement Is Not for Sissies.* Newberg, OR: Barclay Press, 2008.

Morgan, Richard L. *Autumn Wisdom.* Eugene, OR: Wipf and Stock, 2007.

Solin, Daniel R. *The Smartest Retirement Book You'll Ever Need.* New York: Perigee Books, 2009.

Thibault, Jane, and Richard Morgan. *Pilgrimage into the Last Third of Life.* Nashville: Upper Room Books, 2012.

CPSIA information can be obtained
at www.ICGtesting.com
Printed in the USA
BVHW082109270221
601161BV00003B/100